THE GOLF WORLD GUIDE TO BETTER GOLF

THE *GOLF WORLD* GUIDE TO
BETTER GOLF

Foreword by **SEVE BALLESTEROS**

St Michael

The authors are very grateful to the Wentworth Club for allowing
them to use their golf courses for the location photography
contained in the book.

First published 1991

This edition published specially for Marks and Spencer, 1992,
by HarperCollins *Publishers* London.

ISBN 0 583 31395 7

Design and typeset by AB3 Design
Instruction editors: Richard Simmons, John Huggan
Photography: Dave Cannon/Allsport,
Lawrence Levy/Yours in Sport, Jim Moriarty
Illustrations: Dave F. Smith

Typset in Sabon
Printed and bound in Great Britain by
HarperCollins *Manufacturing* Glasgow

Contents

Foreword
by Seve Ballesteros

I have been winning international golf tournaments all around the world since 1976; over 60 of them to date. I have been winning major championships, five so far, since 1979.

My association with *Golf World* magazine, as one of its staff of contributing tournament professionals, only goes back to July 1988, but in the time I have been with *Golf World* I have come to appreciate the professionalism of the magazine's approach, and the strength of its commitment to the presentation of clear, concise golf instruction for its readers. Whether that instruction is passed on by tournament players, such as myself, or by its panel of eminent professional teachers, you can be sure of one thing. The standard of the material is invariably of the highest quality.

That is why I have no hesitation in endorsing this book by four of these teachers: Tommy Horton, whom I have long known from his tournament days;

John Stirling, whose reputation has certainly travelled at least as far as Spain; and Tim Barter and Jim Christine, two of Britain's brightest young golf instructors.

Over recent years, I have collaborated a great deal with both Richard Simmons and John Huggan, the instruction editors, and I am not surprised to see that they have brought to this book the same amount of care and attention that they have always demonstrated in our work together.

We all want to play better golf – me as much as you. I am confident that *The Golf World Guide to Better Golf* will help you do just that.

Severiano Ballesteros
Pedrena
April 1991

Editors' Introduction

The reputation that *Golf World* magazine has achieved since its inception in 1962 has been significantly based upon its commitment to producing high quality pages of instruction. Each month, the magazine devotes up to one-third of its editorial content to making you, the reader, a better golfer.

The calibre of our team is second to none. From the world of tournament golf, Nick Faldo, Greg Norman, Seve Ballesteros, Bernhard Langer, Jack Nicklaus, Curtis Strange and Tom Watson are just a few of the players who regularly contribute their theories and ideas. Throughout the chapters of this book you will find that certain points made in the text are reinforced if you study the pictures that we have included of some of these great players in action.

But that is just half the story. These men are, after all, players and not teachers, and to complement their wealth of invaluable experience, we also lay claim to the service of some of Britain's top teachers. Former captain of the Professional Golfers' Association John Stirling is the senior member of our panel, and for this project he is joined by Ryder Cup veteran Tommy Horton, and fellow PGA professionals Tim Barter and Jim Christine. We hope that you enjoy *The Golf World Guide to Better Golf* – and, of course, that through the pages of this book, their ideas enable you to do just that.

Richard Simmons
John Huggan

The Fundamentals
by John Stirling

The fundamentals represent every golfer's set of rules. The way that you hold the golf club, the way in which you position your body in relation to the ball and the way in which you aim the clubface will determine the outcome of every shot that you hit.

It should come as no surprise to you that most professional golfers throughout the world follow these basic rules to the letter. They spend more time fine-tuning their address position than they do analysing the swing itself. They know full well that the swing is purely a function of their set-up position. You need look no further than Nick Faldo for an example of a player who relentlessly practises the fundamentals. He looks every part a champion, and he sets up to the ball so immaculately that you wonder how he could ever hit a poor shot. As a model for any aspiring young player, or indeed anyone who is serious about improving their game, no-one could

possibly be better than this man.

Most amateur golfers who play only once or twice a week would improve dramatically if they would only spend some time learning about and developing these basics. These mid-and high-handicap golfers worry too much about the swing itself, and pay little attention to the preparation that precedes it. The first lesson that every player must learn is that, in golf, there are no short cuts to success.

Note: the following instructions are written for the right-handed player. The left-handed player must therefore substitute 'left' for 'right' and vice versa.

Aiming the clubface

Your set-up will ultimately determine the accuracy and direction of your swing, so it is vital that it is correct. Following a routine before every shot is the simplest and easiest way to guarantee that you get everything right. I believe that you should aim the clubface before making a grip,

1:1, 1:2 Your aim is crucial. Always study the shot that confronts you before carefully placing the clubface behind the ball along your intended line.

1:3 With the clubface in position, the clubshaft should rest comfortably in front of your body, and you can prepare to make your grip.

but there are many good players who grip the club first, and then aim it. The order is really not that important. What is important is that you satisfy both of these fundamental elements before you do anything else.

First, you must always study the shot that confronts you (**1:1**). Whether you are playing a tee-shot into a narrow fairway or an approach shot into a green, try to visualize the flight of the ball towards your target. Be positive, and build up a picture of the ideal shot in your mind's eye. Then, walk in from behind the ball, and set the bottom front edge of the clubface at right angles to the ball-to-target line (**1:2**).

Your aim is crucial. Look for something on the ground that can help you to position the clubface accurately. Most professionals pick out a secondary target – perhaps an old divot mark or discoloured patch of grass that lies on the ball-to-target line but within the vicinity of the ball – and then aim the clubface at that. It's a lot easier to aim at something

that is close to you than to aim at a target in the distance. Modern irons usually have a white line painted in the first groove, and this serves as a useful point of reference in setting up to the ball correctly.

Finally, in aiming the clubface, make sure that the club sits exactly as the manufacturer intended, with its true loft presented to the back of the ball. Once properly aligned, the clubface will be your main guide in correctly aligning your body to the target-line, so it is vital that this stage in the set-up is done correctly. When the clubface is correctly set, the top of the handle will be roughly opposite the ball, and ready for the placement of the hands.

The grip

Good golf is ball control through clubface control. If you do not take care in establishing a good relationship between your hands and the clubface at address,

1:4, 1:5 The club sits diagonally across the palm of your left hand, with about three-quarters of an inch of the butt end of the grip visible at the top.

then sooner or later you'll run into trouble. The grip represents your only physical contact with the club. It is essential that it is both comfortable and functional.

The grip should be taken with the left hand first (**1:3**). Stand with your arms hanging down by your side in a natural position, your fingertips pointing to the ground, and then place the club across your palm so that it runs diagonally through your hand from the middle of the left forefinger to a point about half to three-quarters of an inch below the base of your little finger (**1:4**). Hold the club so that about three-quarters of an inch of the butt end of the grip protrudes beyond the fleshy pad at the heel of your left hand (**1:5**). If you should grip up the club any higher than this your shortest finger will be wrapped around the thickest part of the grip. Not only is this illogical, but it could lead to a loss of control at the top of your backswing. That's where amateur

players lose the continuity of their swing.

Your grip pressure should be felt mainly in the last three fingers of the left hand. They should secure a firm coupling with the club. Make sure that your hold is firm enough to exercise absolute control over the clubface, but not so tight that you cannot feel the head on the end of the shaft. When all the fingers are closed around the grip, your thumb should sit just to the right of centre on top of the

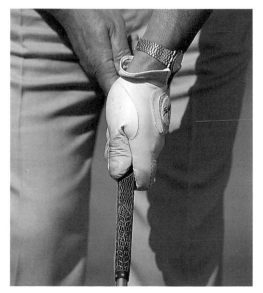

1:6 The 'V' that is formed between your thumb and forefinger should point up towards your right shoulder.

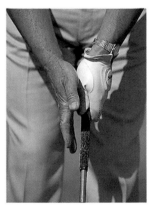

1:7, 1:7a As you introduce your right hand to the club, remember the importance of maintaining a neutral position, and keep your palms facing each other.

shaft, and the 'V' that is formed between your thumb and forefinger should point up towards your right shoulder (**1:6**).

As you bring your right hand to join the left on the grip, remember the importance of maintaining a neutral position (**1:7, 1:7a**). With the left hand already in place, carefully fit the right hand, making sure that the palm of your hand is at right angles to your intended line.

The grip should then be taken within the fingers of the right hand. Think of it like this. Imagine picking up a golf ball as if you were going to throw it a long way. You would hold the ball in the

first three fingers of your right hand, and trigger your right forefinger to enhance your overall feel and control. That's exactly how I believe you should visualize the fit of your right hand. Introduce your hand to the grip so that the club nestles in the channel that is created when you lightly flex your fingers, and in such a way that your left thumb fits snugly beneath the fleshy pad under the base of your right thumb (**1:8**). Your right thumb should rest comfortably to the left of the shaft, and the 'V' that is formed between your thumb and forefinger should again point up towards your right shoulder (**1:9**).

While your left hand largely assumes responsibility for the control of the clubface during the swing, your right hand is the one which transmits power. You should feel a little pressure in your right thumb and forefinger and have the impression in your mind of the right hand whipping the clubhead through impact. Of course, in reality the hands work

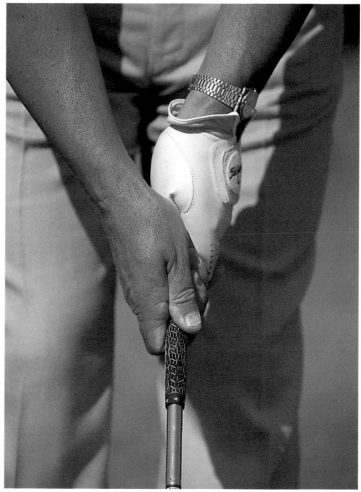

together but you should at least be aware of the relationship between your right hand and the clubhead speed you ultimately create.

The way in which you decide to join your hands together on the grip is very important. Your hands must fit together comfortably so that they are able to work as a unit and maintain control even at great speed.

By far the most popular grip among tournament players is the overlapping, or Vardon grip (**1:10**), in which the little finger of the right hand rides piggy-back on the left forefinger. In

1:8, 1:9 The right hand should fit comfortably beneath the left, and once your grip is completed the 'V's that are formed between the thumb and index finger on each hand should each point towards your right shoulder.

so doing, this overlap reinforces the control that the left hand has over the clubhead, while at the same time preserving that element of feel within the right hand. The little finger can sit either on top of the exposed knuckle of the left forefinger, or it can rest neatly in the groove that is formed between the left forefinger and middle finger. You must find the position which feels most comfortable and which suits your style of play.

Alternatively, you might like to experiment with the interlocking grip – as used by Jack Nicklaus and many other great players – entwining the little finger of your right hand with the forefinger of your left (**1:11**). This particular style is not as widely used as the overlapping grip, but it is popular with players who have smaller hands and fingers, and who find stretching their little finger to make the overlap a little too uncomfortable. I believe the interlocking grip to be inferior to the overlapping, for the simple reason that when you interlock your fingers you lose the service of your left forefinger on the shaft. This is a strong finger, and it should play an important role in maintaining clubhead control with the left hand. With the overlapping grip your left forefinger remains on the shaft, and its position is then further reinforced when you make the overlap with your little finger.

The baseball grip, where you have all eight fingers on the club, is a third possible choice (**1:12**). With this grip the hands are free to work much more independently, and for that reason it is a grip that I recommend only for weaker players, beginners and juniors, who need as much help as they can get to generate clubhead speed. The baseball grip serves as a good starter-grip, but it should be substituted for a more orthodox interlocking or overlapping grip as soon as a level of proficiency is reached if further improvement is to follow.

Whichever style you prefer, it is important that you assemble your grip with your palms facing each other, and in such a way that each hand is square to the target-line. Neither hand should be turned too far to the left or too far to the right. So placed, the hands are in a neutral position on the club. In the final analysis, you should be able to look down upon your completed grip and see at least two knuckles on the back of your left

hand and the first knuckle on the back of your right (**1:13**). This is generally accepted as being orthodox. So placed, the hands are in a neutral position on the club. And it has been anatomically proved that they return to this neutral position at impact, regardless of their position at address. That's why you must establish a perfectly square relationship between your hands and the clubface before you go on to work on your swing.

Grip lightly for 'feel'

Earlier, I used the analogy of picking up and throwing a golf ball with your right hand to help clarify what I believe to be the correct position of the right hand on the grip. That same throwing analogy can also help you to understand the importance of your grip pressure.

Your grip pressure is one of the keys to a free, uninhibited swing. If you were going to throw a ball any great distance, you would instinctively hold it quite lightly in your fingers so that the muscles in your hands and arms were free of tension and able to generate speed. Your body would be keyed up in anticipation of making a powerful athletic movement, but it would at the same time be relaxed.

The golf swing is no different. Both your grip and set-up position must be designed with this flowing athletic movement in mind. Preparation is the key. It is important that you get 'ready' to swing, and this ready position stems

1:13 In the final analysis, it should be possible to look down upon your completed grip and see at least two knuckles on the back of your left hand, and the first knuckle on the back of your right.

15

largely from your grip. It must be firm enough to maintain control over the clubhead, but not so tight that you effectively stifle the movement of your hands and arms. Learn to hold the club with a light, sensitive grip, one that allows you to really feel the clubhead on the end of the shaft. That will enable you to swing with the utmost power and control.

Common faults

Any discrepancy that exists between the alignment of your hands and the clubface at address will inevitably be reflected at impact. As I mentioned earlier, it has been proved that your hands return to a neutral position at impact regardless of their position at address, and so any fault that you have will be transmitted down through the shaft to the clubface, and ultimately to the ball.

If, for example, you play with a hooker's grip, with each hand turned too far to the right on the club at address (**1:14, 1:14a**), then the result at impact will be a clubface that has its toe

1:14, 1:14a, 1:15
If you play with a hooker's grip, in which the hands are turned too far to the right on the club at address, then the result will be a closed clubface at impact, spinning the ball from right to left.

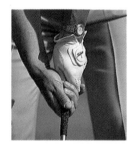

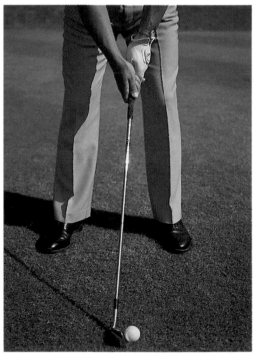

turned inwards. Your hands will simply return to a neutral position, clearly exposing your set-up fault (**1:15**).

Conversely, if you play with a slicer's grip, with your hands turned too far to the left on the club (**1:16, 1:16a**), then the clubface will be open when it returns to the ball, imparting cutspin (**1:17**).

If you suffer with either of these common faults it is quite likely that you will try to compensate for the devastating effect that it has on the clubface at impact with a series of incorrect movements during your swing. This only makes matters worse. Faults to cure faults simply complicate the issue. It's far better to work back and trace the real cause of your trouble, and the grip is undoubtedly one of the key fundamentals to good golf.

Ball position

I teach the ball position within a three-ball span (**1:18**). Playing the ball from just opposite the inside of your left heel will promote the sweeping action through

1:16, 1:16a, 1:17
A slicer's grip, with the hands turned too far to the left on the club at address, inevitably leaves the clubface open at impact, spinning the ball away weakly from left to right.

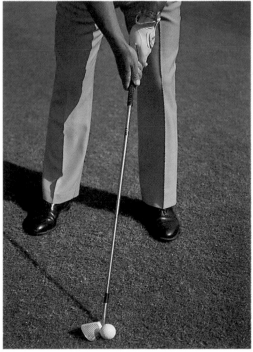

impact that you need in order to produce a good clean strike and a penetrating ball flight. That's the position that I would recommend for all your wood and long iron shots, up to the 4-iron. But as you move down through the irons the strike you want will vary. With a medium iron you should endeavour to strike the ball as you approach the very bottom of your arc, the clubhead travelling parallel to the

1:18 For the differing strikes that you should strive to achieve, I recommend that you vary your ball position within a three-ball span.

ground after impact and only lightly brushing the grass in front of the ball. The middle ball represents the ideal position for these medium iron shots, the 5-, 6- and 7- irons. Finally, play your short iron shots from the position of the right hand ball. Here, the ball will be met as the clubhead is descending, and that will help you establish a positive ball-turf strike which produces maximum backspin.

You can – and indeed you should –

experiment with this. Some players arrive at the bottom of their arc earlier or later than others. It all depends on the shape of your swing and your physical capabilities. Have a few practice swings and find out exactly where the bottom of your swing falls with each club. That will then enable you to gauge the correct ball position that suits your play.

The parallel alignment factors

Aiming the clubface correctly gets you only halfway to your ultimate goal of aiming your swing correctly. That's what your set-up is all about. Now you must aim your body, and that involves aligning your feet, knees, hips and shoulders on a line that is parallel to the target line. In this position your body will be ideally placed to produce an effective swing, one that delivers the clubface squarely and consistently to the back of the ball.

Before I explain to you the concept of these parallel alignment factors, there's a misconception regarding the position of your body at address that must be cleared up right away.

When you aim a golf club, you do exactly that. You aim the clubface squarely at the target and then relate your body position to the clubface. You do not aim your body at the target. Think about it. At address you are standing to the left of the ball as you view the target, and your body must naturally be set parallel to your target-line, and so in effect, aimed to the left of the target itself. The reason why so many amateur players finish up to the right of their target is that they aim their body at the target – believing that to be the correct thing to do – and then drop the clubface behind the ball. Quite obviously, this is not the case.

The easiest way to check your body alignment at address is to lay clubs on the ground that correspond with your target-line. Try to establish a routine whenever you practise. First, lay a club down behind the ball in line with your target (**1:19**). Then place another club six to eight inches outside the ball, exactly parallel to the first (**1:20**). Finally, remove the club that is directly behind the ball and replace it inside the ball, parallel to the outer club. These two clubs will now help you to set up correctly, aligning both the clubface and your body squarely to the target-line (**1:21**).

Familiarize yourself with the feeling of being square by practising regularly in this position. If you have access to a full-length mirror, then stand in front of it and check that your feet, knees, hips and shoulders are in parallel. Your alignment is crucial.

As I mentioned earlier, the professionals practise the fundamentals relentlessly. If there is a secret to playing consistently good golf, then that's it. At any tournament you will find them rigorously checking their alignment in this very way. It's simple, but it's effective. I

1:19, 1:20, 1:21 Whenever you practise, it is vital that you first lay clubs on the ground to check your ball position and body alignment.

cannot over-emphasize the importance of establishing this linear relationship between your feet, knees, hips and shoulders.

Posture

Posture refers to the overall position of your body at address. Since it has a lot to do with the way in which you ultimately swing the golf club, it's logical that you should adopt a posture that will help you to swing the way you want. A good posture will not only place your body in a position from which the arms can swing freely and in the correct plane, but it will at the same time assist in helping you to maintain your balance and shift your

1:22, 1:23
A normal walking pace is a good guide to ascertaining the width of stance that you should adopt for the full swing.

weight correctly during the swing. Although this is a static position, it must be geared towards producing fluent motion. You can make the task of attaining the proper posture a little easier by using clubs whose lengths and lies are suited to you. Correctly fitted clubs will help you to create the correct spine angle simply by grounding the club, flexing your knees and balancing your body.

A good posture requires that you first establish a firm foundation. The width of your stance can be arrived at quite easily if you take a normal walking pace leading with your left foot (**1:22**), and then turning through 90 degrees (**1:23**). Doing this results in a width of stance that is geared specifically to your leg length. The outsides of your feet should be slightly wider than your shoulders, and you should feel that your weight is centred over the balls of your feet.

The angles that you create at address are designed to help move your body correctly and produce an effective swing. Obviously there has to be a degree of bending over if you are to assemble a position that is capable of delivering the clubface consistently back to the ball. With your knees and thigh muscles flexed, bend over gently from the hips, and at the same time stick your bottom out (**1:24** and **1:24a**). Don't sit down or topple forwards, but assume a comfortable, athletic posture. Again, check your body position in a mirror. Make sure that your

1:24, 1:24a *The angles that you create at address are designed to help you move your body correctly and produce an effective swing. Check your position regularly in a mirror, and work on assuming an athletic position.*

lower back is kept relatively aligned. You should be able to feel a certain amount of tension in your thighs as your legs are keyed up to support the swing.

Once your body is in a good position, your arms should be free to hang from your shoulders, placing your hands somewhere approximately beneath your chin (**1:25**). They should be extended comfortably without being stiffened. Your left arm should feel that it is the more prominent at address, and as such, this establishes the radius of your swing. Your right arm should be relaxed, slightly lower than the left, and ready to fold neatly away in the backswing.

The distance that you must stand away from the ball will be determined quite naturally by the length of the shaft

of whatever club you are using. Your posture in terms of the relationship between your arms and your body should remain consistent, although your spine angle must be flexible enough to accommodate the varying length of each shaft.

The angle at which each club sits will of course vary, and you must make certain that the clubhead sits as the manufacturer intended. The longer-shafted driver (**1:26**) has the flattest lie of all your clubs, and will require that you stand a little further away from the ball than you would with a pitching wedge (**1:27**). As you stand further away from the ball so your spine angle will be eased. The shorter clubs are designed to sit in a more upright position, bringing your body gradually closer to the ball, and require that you bend over a little more from the hips. You must learn to trust the lie of each club and adjust your position at address accordingly. The success of your swing depends on it.

Finally, let me stress again the importance of having correctly fitted clubs. They will help you to eliminate much of the uncertainty that surrounds posture, and help you get into a position at address that is not only comfortable, but dynamic and effective.

1:25 Even without a club you can practise getting into a good position at address. Work on keeping your back relatively straight, bend over from the hips and flex your knees for a comfortable 'ready' position.

*1:26, 1:27 The longer shafted driver (**above**) has the flattest lie of all your clubs, and will require that you stand a little further away from the ball than you would with the more steeply angled pitching wedge (**left**).*

The Full Swing
by Tommy Horton

Golf swings are like fingerprints; no two are the same. They may start from the same position – every player needs the sound fundamentals described in the previous chapter – but soon after the club moves away from the ball differences become clear.

Those differences are apparent even at impact. All golf swings do not arrive at impact looking the same. Only players attempting to hit the same shape of shot will closely resemble each other at impact.

What is important about impact is that it mirrors as closely as possible your address position (**2:1, 2:2**). That is where you want to return with the clubhead travelling squarely through the ball to the target. Of course, it is not really possible to reproduce exactly 'address at impact': impact is, after all, a position *within motion*, but it is a good thought to have. A thought that will help you reproduce that impact position as often as possible while knowing what happens when you

err. That, in turn, allows you to be reasonably sure of your ball flight and shape of shot. You can draw, fade or hit the ball straight – the choice is yours.

The trick is knowing yourself and your capabilities well enough to choose the method and ball flight best for you. Every great player has successfully accomplished that feat. They have not wasted time trying to be someone else. Their games are built around two things: solid fundamentals and an honest appraisal of their capabilities. That is important. Your temperament is just as much a part of your game as your grip.

The best competitors are those whose blend of swing, psychological profile and physical make-up is best suited to them. Take Lee Trevino, for example (**2:3**). Lee learned very early in his career that he was never going to swing the club in anything like a classic manner. But he built a method ideally suited to his physical capabilities and

2:1, 2:2 Although a position within motion, your impact position should, as closely as possible, mirror your address position.

personality. A method that he could repeat under the severest pressure. That must be your goal too.

Look at it this way. The golfing gods are a capricious lot, not given to surrendering their favours for more than a few moments at a time. How often have you walked off an 18th green with 'the secret' only to return twenty-four short hours later to find it gone as quickly as it arrived? Consistency is an elusive thing.

So be realistic. Although top players spend all their time trying to hit great shots, they also recognize that more shots are mis-hit than struck perfectly. That is true for everyone. Every golfer who has ever played mis-hits, however

slightly, seven shots out of ten. It is simply the quality of the mis-hits that separates winners from losers. Watch Nick Faldo hit ten shots and they all look pretty much the same. You can't tell his good ones from his bad ones. And those superior mis-hits separate him from the rest of the field.

Do you want to move closer to that ideal? Or are you content to stay at your present level, living with the same old faults and playing defensive golf? If you want to break out of that mould, you need to make some decisions about the way you want to play the game.

What shape of shot do you want? Be clear about that before you set up to the ball. Don't fall into the trap I see so often at teaching schools. A lot of people practise their backswings thoughtlessly. They have very little idea as to where they want the ball to start and finish. They don't have a clear picture in their minds. They are bogged down in what I call negative instruction. They are trying to avoid doing something wrong. What they should be working on, of course, is what they have to do right. Knowing what you are doing wrong is of little use to you. So concentrate only on the drills which will help your game. Be positive. You have to visualize shots before you hit them. If you want to hit a draw the ball must start to the right; a fade and the ball must start left.

Unfortunately, most players have too much curvature on their shots. Those fades and draws are slices and hooks. If you fall into either category, work back to a middle road. Take things slowly. You will never turn a banana slice into a draw in five minutes. It takes time. If you slice the ball too much, try to take just some of that left-to-right flight out of your shots. Not all of it. To go from a big slice to a straight shot or a draw is too drastic. Because you will probably still be aiming left to allow for a slice, you end up unsure on the course. After years of watching your shots curve from left-to-right, you don't visualize a draw in your mind's eye. The result is confusion.

Never think of your swing as anything but a swing. It is not a series of movements; it is a *swing*. Again, be clear about what you are trying to do. If you tend to swing the club flat with your hands lower than your right shoulder at the end of your backswing (**2:4**), picture in your mind someone like Jack Nicklaus (**2:5**). His high hand action is what you should be working towards. Equally, if your backswing is on the upright side

2:3 Lee Trevino's flat, laid-off backswing is indicative of the fact that he has always felt most comfortable playing with the low, left-to-right shaped shot.

2:4, 2:5, 2:6, 2:7
Visualizing the swing of a great player in the back of your mind can often help you to overcome a fault. If, for example, your swing tends to be on the flat side, picture the high hand action of Jack Nicklaus. Equally, if your backswing is too upright, then Paul Azinger's flat backswing – minus his open stance – is a good model for you.

(**2:6**), Paul Azinger (minus his open stance) is a good model for you (**2:7**).

Let's start at the beginning.

The takeaway

I believe that the best way for the backswing to start can be summed up in one word: togetherness. The club, your torso, your arms and your shoulders must correspondingly extravagant move to the right. The chances of you reproducing your address position at impact are then drastically reduced. If head movement is a problem for you, focus on the back of the ball. That is, after all, where you want the club to make contact. If you look at the top of the ball, there is a fair chance that is where the club will arrive,

2:8, 2:8a The club, your torso, your arms and your shoulders must all move away from the ball together in what is commonly referred to as a one-piece takeaway.

all move together in what is commonly called a one-piece takeaway (**2:8, 2:8a**). (I define the takeaway as being that part of the swing which moves the club from address to a point where the shaft is horizontal.) Almost every great player you care to mention starts his swing in this way. So should you.

Even your head shifts a little as the club moves away from the ball. But only a little. Excessive head movement can only lead to your body making a so look at the part you want to hit.

Then turn your chin slightly to the right, keeping it off your chest. Your shoulders need that room in which to turn. If your chin is slumped on your chest, your shoulders have nowhere to go and you cannot make a proper turn.

When you make a one-piece takeaway, your swing is off to the best possible start. You are co-ordinated and fully in control of every aspect of your swing. Unco-ordinated swings occur

2:9, 2:10, 2:11 Swinging a club with your feet together is a good test of just how co-ordinated and balanced your swing is.

because one part of the body moves faster than another. Don't think that a slow swing is necessarily good. I hear all the time from pupils that they are 'all right if I slow down'. Well, that is simply not true. If you can't swing reasonably briskly then there is something wrong with your method. In fact, if your mechanics are good, you can swing almost as fast as you like.

If you have trouble making a smooth, co-ordinated takeaway, make some swings with your feet together (**2:9, 2:10, 2:11**). That forces you to swing smoothly. If you don't, you will fall over! The unco-ordinated culprit – be it club, torso, arms, shoulders or legs – will soon show up. When it does, work on speeding up those parts that are moving slowly. That is better than slowing down

2:12, 2:13, 2:14, 2:15, 2:15a From the point where the clubshaft is horizontal, your wrists curl in conjuncti with your body-turn to carry the club all the way to the top of the backswing.

those that are already setting the pace. Always build up the part that is not moving well.

Curl your wrists to the top

When the shaft of your club reaches the point where it is horizontal (and parallel with the ball-target line) something has to give. And that something is your wrists. From that point, around halfway through your backswing, your wrists must curl in order for the club to get back to horizontal (or close to it) at the top of your swing (**2.12, 2:13, 2:14, 2:15, 2:15a**).

I call this motion 'curling' because I dislike the terms 'breaking' or 'cocking'. To me they convey looseness and inconsistency. Curling is a firmer, less floppy and more repeatable swing key.

Understand too that as the biggest muscles in your body are controlling the clubhead on the way back, they are also turning your hips. Take care though. Your hips don't turn nearly as much as your shoulders. About 45 degrees in the hips compared with a 90-degree shoulder-turn is about right. But you shouldn't have to think of that too much. Focus on the flex you introduced in your knees at address, particularly in the right leg.

Your weight settles onto your right side as your backswing progresses. And as your shoulders and hips turn, your left hip is pulled around with your left knee (which should point at the ground a little behind the ball). The key is maintaining the flex in your right knee throughout (**2:16, 2:17**).

Turn around it. The knee's stability prevents any possibility of you swaying off the ball to the right. Your weight should then be concentrated primarily on your right heel. The last

backswing movement occurs in your left heel. It either comes off the ground or rolls over slightly, depending on your level of flexibility.

At this point, I would like to mention that much-misunderstood term 'swing plane'. A good swing plane results from the proper blending of arm action and shoulder turn. It's that simple. If your arms swing but your shoulders don't turn, then your swing will not be 'on plane'. This is true no matter what club you have in your hands. The only difference is that a driver (**2:18**) will automatically give you a flatter swing plane than a wedge (**2:18a**). Because a driver has a longer shaft and flatter lie than a wedge, you stand further away from the ball. So your swing is more rounded.

2:16, 2:17 Maintain the flex in your right knee throughout the backswing.

2:18, 2:18a Each club in the bag has a slightly different loft and lie, and this will determine the plane of your swing. A driver, for example, with its longer shaft and flatter lie, will automatically give you a flatter swing plane than a wedge, which is a shorter club, and quite naturally sits at a much steeper angle.

To summarize, the whole backswing is a chain reaction set off by a one-piece start, everything working together. Then your shoulders gain control, turning your body around your right knee to the top. Think of it as shoulders, hips, knees, feet.

Coming down again

The key to your whole golf swing is the start of your downswing. It is the single most difficult move in your whole action. That may sound daunting, but think of it in these terms: what moves last on the way back must move first on the way down. So the left heel is the first thing to shift back by returning to its original position (**2:19**).

That sets off another chain reaction. Once your heel is back on the ground, your left knee and left hip return to their starting positions. These moves align your feet and hips squarely with the ball-target line. And as the knee and hips move, your upper body starts its movement with your arms swinging the

2:19, 2:20 The change in direction is arguably the single most important move in your swing. As the left heel returns to its original starting position, the left knee and hip rotate back towards the target and the arms are free to swing the clubhead down towards the ball from inside the ball-to-target line.

*2:21, 2:22 The shoulders move last, and come into play only in response to the unwinding of the lower body (**right**). If the downswing is initiated by the shoulders the only space available to your arms and the club is outside the ball-to-target line, which is disastrous (**far right**).*

club down in the space created by the fully-turned shoulders (**2:20**). In that way the club approaches the ball from inside the ball-target line (**2:21**).

The most important thing is that your shoulders move last. They only come into play as a result of the action in your legs, hips and arms. If your downswing is started by your shoulders, then the whole action is ruined. The only space available to your arms and the club is then outside the ball-target line (**2:22**). You will come 'over the top' with the club approaching the ball from outside the line. The result is a slice if your clubface happens to be square or open to the target; a straight pull if the clubface is closed. Either way, you're headed for trouble.

If this, or a corresponding hook, is your golfing curse, work on creating this

order of things on the downswing: heel, knee, hips, arms, shoulders. Get your local professional or someone who knows your swing well to check your progress.

Through to the finish

The important word here is *through*. The golf swing is not a backswing, a downswing and a follow- through. It is a backswing and a through swing. The club meets the ball as it is travelling to the target. You don't stop at impact. Your left side must continue to rotate without sliding laterally. The rest of your body then follows that lead until the club returns above your head.

Again there is a proper order of things. As your body continues to rotate after impact, your left knee holds. When the club is passing waist height, your stomach will already be facing the target.

Your arms and shoulders then continue to turn until the club is over your left shoulder, to the left of your left ear. They are, in effect, opposite to where they were at the top of your backswing. You should finish with your weight concentrated on your left heel and the toe of your right foot (**2:23**).

That sounds complex, but if you have made a good swing through impact it should all happen automatically. Make many practice swings at half speed in order to feel your whole action. And don't waste these swings. Always aim to hit something on the ground. That gives you some feedback on how good a practice swing you have made. If you are not aiming at anything, you can't tell how good your swing was.

Remember that the ball gets in the way of a good swing. Don't think of your through swing as an attack on the ball. Forget any desire to hit 'at' the ball, make a *swing*. Try to feel the swinging of the clubhead from address to finish. Use a weighted club or a weight on the end of a piece of string to enhance your awareness of the clubhead (**2:24, 2:25**). Again, move slowly. You have to swing smoothly; you can't swing fast. This is the best exercise I know for your golfing muscles.

2:23, 2:24, 2:25 *A good follow-through position is simply the inevitable result of all the good moves that went on before, and you should finish with your weight concentrated on your left heel and balanced on the toe of your right foot. To help you to become familiar with this position, try training with a weighted club. It is one of the most effective exercises that I know for a good golf swing.*

The driver swing
GREG NORMAN

Loading the big gun (the backswing)

There is nothing more satisfying in golf than to stand on a tee and sweep the ball away solidly down the middle of the fairway with a driver. Greg Norman knows that more than most. Not only is he long, but more importantly he is accurate, giving him a tremendous advantage on those courses where length is a prime factor.

The address position is a matter of comfort and common sense. If your stance is too narrow you won't have enough stability to make a full, wide swing away from the ball. On the other hand, if your stance is too wide, you'll inhibit your ability to make a good shoulder-turn. Either way, you'll lose power. The standard rule for the drive is that your stance should be about the same width as your shoulders.

The most important move when it comes to driving the ball consistently straight and true is the takeaway, and it is worth noting just how well Greg has maintained the relationship between his arms and wrists over the first few feet of his backswing as a result of his smooth one-piece takeaway. 'Low and slow' are the key words to describe the proper takeaway, and you should try to emulate Greg, and glide the clubhead away from the ball. A full backswing depends mostly on your ability to turn away from the ball. You must try to turn your hips and shoulders so that, at the top of your swing, your back faces the target. Greg's overriding swing-thought is 'right pocket back', and you can clearly see the effect that this has. Turning his right front trouser pocket around to the back as far as possible has ensured a good hip-turn. And when the hips turn, the back and shoulders turn. The position that Greg achieves at the top is one that we should all be trying to achieve – the fully coiled, high-armed, powerful action of a world-class player.

Driving down to impact
(the downswing)

The correct leg-action is essential in generating power: the left leg and hip initiating the downswing with a lateral move to the left, back to where they were at address. The left knee moves laterally into the forward swing and pulls on the left hip, which in turn pulls the left arm downwards. At the same time, the right knee begins to drive towards the target, taking with it the shoulders, arms and hands, bringing the club down towards the ball on an inside path.

When you execute the swing correctly, this leadership of the lower body creates a lag of the hands and the clubhead, resulting in what's commonly called a delayed release. In this position, just prior to impact, the wrists have not uncocked, and there is a tremendous amount of clubhead speed ready to be unleashed.

In a good swing the position at impact is very similar to the position at address, although as impact is a position within motion there are obvious differences. Once past impact there's little that you can do to influence the flight of the ball, but since a good follow-through is the result of a sound swing, it pays to know what the proper finish looks like.

Our final picture shows the full-flowing, powerful finish of a very strong and confident man. A high finish, full body-turn and athletic leg and footwork make this action the reward for a great backswing and powerful release of energy through the ball.

The 7-iron swing
BERNHARD LANGER

Turning into a strong backswing

For pin-point accuracy from the fairway, your approach to every approach shot has to be exact. Bernhard Langer is renowned for the accuracy of his iron play, and as he clearly illustrates in this sequence, making the full use of your body-turn is the most reliable way to produce a compact and powerful swing.

At address, Langer adopts a position in which his body is square to the target, and he spreads his weight evenly between his feet. You will notice that his left arm and the clubshaft form a straight line – here he is using a 7-iron – and it is this relationship that he establishes at address that will form the radius of his swing. Langer, who has always played with a very strong left hand grip, gets his swing off to a good start with an early rotation of his knees and hips. He makes a smooth, wide takeaway , and paves the way towards a strong shoulder-turn. At the top of his backswing his left shoulder is under his chin, and both his back and the clubshaft face the target. He has loaded his backswing with a full 90-degree shoulder-turn and a 45-degree hip-turn, coiling the large muscles of his body. The downswing is all set to be a natural recoiling of that stored energy.

Pulling down the line

During the backswing Bernhard's weight is transferred to the right side of his body, being supported by his right leg, particularly the right knee, but as he starts the downswing that weight now shifts back onto the left side. The important thing in the downswing is to have the arms, legs and the body working as one unit, moving together back towards the ball.

One way to ensure that everything works back towards the ball together is to feel that you pull the butt end of the grip (i.e. the top of it) towards the ball as you pull the club down. That's a swing-thought that Langer has often worked with, and it helps him to stay behind the shot at impact. Through the ball his weight transfers over onto his left side as he continues to drive his legs forward, and he completes his follow-through with a well-balanced finish.

If you find that you are struggling to get the club on the correct inside path on the downswing, then the fault will often be due to a lack of proper leg-work – a failure to shift the body's weight on to the left side in the downswing, thereby blocking the club's path back to the ball. If this sounds a familiar problem to you, then make a mental note of Langer's swing: work on your hip- and shoulder- turn in the backswing, and then release your body coil with a strong, athletic leg-action in the downswing and on into the follow-through.

From 100 yards in
by Jim Christine

The chief objective in golf is to get the ball into the hole in as few shots as possible, but I am amazed at how many experienced players lose sight of this basic fact. For them the golf course is a place in which to play 'golf swing' rather than golf. They wrap themselves in theory, content to hit two or three great shots in a round rather than make a good score.

Sometimes these golfers have passable long games, but invariably their short games let them down. Their obsession with full-swing mechanics hurts their ability to score. From 100 yards in to the flag, these poor unfortunates waste more shots than they ever save. The net result is that they are not winners. They 'lose pretty' rather than 'win ugly'. Make sure you never fall into that trap. Never imagine that the little guy who beat you on the last green by chipping and putting his way round was lucky. He wasn't. He knew that winning is about scoring well.

That, then, is the aim of this chapter: to save you shots in the most important area of the course, from 100 yards in to the flag. You do, after all, hit upwards of 70 per cent of your shots from inside that range.

The first thing to realize about playing these shots is that rhythm and balance are your most important attributes. Strength and brute force have little part to play.

The closer you get to the hole the less power you need, so you have to create smaller swings. These swings have their own fundamentals. You have to build a method that is in tune with the length of swing you want to make.

The biggest contrast occurs when you move from a pitch shot to a chip shot. A chip shot is played with little or no wrist action or transfer of weight. It is basically a hands and arms shot; an extension of a long putt. The pitch shot, being longer, requires you to create more clubhead speed by transferring your weight and using your wrists.

Let's work our way towards the green from 100 yards out.

The full wedge

One of the keys to a successful short game is knowing how far you can hit a full wedge shot. Every good player knows this, and so should you.

If you find that a comfortably played shot with your wedge goes 95 yards, try to get yourself in a position to play that shot as often as possible. Try to hit your ball 95 yards from the flag. Good players do that. They don't thoughtlessly hit to 70 yards at one hole, 85 at the next and 60 at the one after that. They know that they can be more aggressive and score better when most of

their short approach shots are played from around 95 yards.

You can be more aggressive too, but take care. You are not as good as the professionals, so don't attack every flag. Give yourself more margin for error, even if that means aiming a few yards left or right on occasion.

Don't worry that someone else hits a full wedge shot further than you. Don't compare yourself with anyone else. Pure distance is not what this shot is about. This is a scoring shot. It is about getting used to the length *you* hit the ball. Your goal is to be able to hit say ten wedge

3:1 To play the pitch shot, align your knees, hips and shoulders as you would normally, parallel to your ball-to-target line.

3:2 The ball is played from inside the left heel, with your hands just ahead of the ball.

shots within five yards of each other. It is *not* to acquire the ability to occasionally hit one 135 yards.

To that end, a full wedge shot never requires more than a three-quarter swing. And the way to create that slightly shorter swing starts at address.

Align everything – your shoulders, hips and club – as you would normally, parallel to the ball-target line with your feet a little open (aligned left) and a little closer together than if your were hitting a mid-iron (**3:1**). That will automatically restrict your ability to turn your right side away from the ball and so shorten your swing. Place the ball a little inside your left heel, your hands just ahead of the ball (**3:2**). There is no need to push your hands forward excessively. That only delofts the club. Grip lightly but firmly. Place a little more weight on your left side. A 60/40 weight distribution between your left foot and right foot is about what you need to encourage the necessary downward path of the club through impact.

Start your swing smoothly (**3:3**). Think 'tempo'. You're going to be hitting within yourself, so why rush? When your hands move back to a point opposite your right knee, your wrists should start to break. Let the weight of the club tell you exactly when.

Maintain the smoothness you

3:3, 3:4, 3:4a Swing the club back smoothly and feel your weight shift onto your right side as you reach the top of your swing.

3:5, 3:5a Focus on your foot and leg action as you change direction. Transfer your weight back onto your left side smoothly and let your arms swing freely.

3:6 A smooth transfer of weight will produce a smooth swing of the clubhead through impact.

introduced at address all the way to the top (**3:4, 3:4a**). Don't waste time focusing on your weight shift; you are not hitting a driver. If you swing back in balance, you should attain a good position without too much conscious thought.

Smoothness is again your watchword when you change direction. Begin in your lower body (**3:5, 3:5a**). Focus on your feet; let them dictate the pace of your forward swing. Transfer your weight from your right shoe to your left shoe. Be light on your feet. Swing your arms freely and allow them to follow the lead of your legs. If you shift your weight smoothly, then swinging the clubhead equally smoothly through impact will follow as a matter of course.

The club will get the ball airborne for you (**3:6**). It is designed to hit high shots, so there is no need to flick at the ball with your hands and arms in order to lift the ball into the air. That only leads to inconsistency of flight and distance. Remember, you are trying to hit this shot the same distance every time.

Your follow-through should closely mirror your backswing in terms of length (**3:7, 3:7a**). The club is never moving at

3:7, 3:7a Balance is your watchword in the follow-through. Contain your swing with good footwork and finish with the club held comfortably above your left shoulder.

3:8, 3:8a To play a slightly shorter pitch, keep your body lines parallel to the ball-to-target line, but open up your feet a little more and place them closer together.

top speed so there is no need to wrap the shaft around your neck. Stay balanced.

The pitch shot

As you get closer to the hole, the arc of your swing gets smaller. That's how you control the distance the ball travels. You don't keep making the same three-quarter swing at a slower pace. Hitting a solid shot when the clubhead is decelerating into impact is difficult to gauge consistently.

Maintain the rhythm and tempo you used for the full wedge shot when pitching. Again, the way you set up to the ball will help you achieve that.

Just as you narrowed and opened your stance for the wedge, do the same again for a shorter pitch shot. Keep your body lines parallel to the ball-target line, but open your feet up a little more and place them closer together (**3:8, 3:8a**). Only when you are playing a particularly high shot, one where you have to open the face of the club, should your shoulders move away from square. But as long as the clubface is square, so should your shoulders be.

This further opening and narrowing of your stance restricts your swing even more than before so making a shorter swing both back and through should be no problem (**3:9, 3:10, 3:11**). Help yourself by gripping down the club if you have to. Basically, this swing is a mini-version of your full wedge shot.

3:9, 3:10, 3:11 These adjustments will serve to restrict the length of your swing, which will otherwise be similar to that which you use for the full pitch.

The chip shot

All pitch shots involve some use of your wrists and some transfer of your weight. Chip shots don't. They are played with firm wrists and no transfer of weight. Your hands and arms dominate the stroke. Because of that, it is impossible to hit a chip shot very far. So for most players any shot within 20 yards of the pin is a chip.

A chip is really just an extension of a long putt. Think of it as a long putt played with a club that has loft. I recommend that you use the following clubs for chipping: sand wedge, wedge, 9-iron, 8-iron and 7-iron. They will cover almost every situation you are likely to encounter. I see little point in trying to manufacture different shots with a single club. That's too difficult. Make things easy for yourself. Learn one swing with five different clubs rather than varying your swing with one club.

As you narrowed and opened your stance for a pitch shot, so you must do again for a chip. The vast majority of your weight should now be concentrated on your left foot (**3:12**). That will encourage the slight downward hit you need to make solid contact between club and ball. Keep things simple. Swing normally and accelerate smoothly through the ball. Your follow-through should be the same length as your backswing (**3:13, 3:14**).

Good chipping comes from that old standby – practice. You have to experiment with your chipping clubs so that you know what each one can do in any given situation (**3.15**). Within that, however, there are some rules you should follow:

3:12, 3:13, 3:14
Think of the chip shot as being merely an extension of the putting stroke. Gripping the club down the shaft for extra control, concentrate on making a simple back-and-through swing, clipping the ball cleanly with minimal wrist action.

sand
iron 9iron 7iron

(1) I see a chip shot played with a 7-iron as consisting of one third air travel and two thirds over land. A 9-iron shot is 50/50. And a sand wedge is two thirds through the air and one third along the ground. Use that as the basis for all your shots. Be flexible, but I think you'll visualize your shots more clearly if you never stray too far from these guidelines.

(2) Concentrate on distance rather than directional control. Imagine you are chipping down a corridor six feet wide (**3:16**). Anyone can do that. All you have to worry about is your distance. Direction is taken care of. Make yourself a corridor by placing some clubs on the green between you and the hole. Then practise chipping down that chute. You'll soon improve your feel for pace and distance.

(3) Always, if you can, land your

3:16 Distance is often harder to gauge than direction. Imagine you are chipping down a narrow corridor – laying clubs on the green will help you – and concentrate only on distance.

3:15 As long as you develop a simple, repetitive stroke, the only thing that will alter the flight of the ball is the loft on the club that you elect to use. A chip shot played with a 7-iron, for example, will consist of one-third air travel and two-thirds over land, while a sand iron will fly the ball further through the air but upon landing there will be less roll. It is up to you to experiment with all of the options available.

ball on the green. Putting surfaces are generally flatter than their surrounds and offer a more predictable first bounce. Always know where you want the ball to land before you take the club back. Pick your spot. Lay some clubs or pieces of wood on the green at five feet intervals (**3:17**). Attempt to land your ball between the first and second club, then the second and third and so on. Change clubs after every few shots.

(4) Vary your practice. Chipping with the same club to the same hole has limited value because you get used to the

3:17 One way to enhance your feel for the distance that you carry the ball onto the green is by practising this ladder-drill. Lay some clubs on the green at five feet intervals, and attempt to land your ball between the first, then the second, the third and so on.

distance and you get bored. So mix things up. Chip to different holes. Change clubs often. And pay attention to the trajectory and roll each club produces. That is real practice.

(5) Know that where you grip each club varies with the length of shaft each possesses. Hold your 7-iron at the bottom of the grip; the 9-iron halfway up; and the sand wedge as you would for a full shot. Don't be too dogmatic, however. Be prepared to experiment, even to the extent of trying your putting grip on occasion.

These are the basics of wedge play, pitching and chipping. But, of course, golf is not quite that predictable a game. Not every shot will fall into such tidy little categories. Sometimes you are going to be faced with a shot that needs to be hit higher or lower, with spin, from a divot, from a tight lie, or from the rough. Let's look at some of these more specialized shots.

Higher and lower

The simplest way to hit the ball higher is to adjust your address position. It is a good rule of thumb when you are trying to hit a shot a particular way to make any changes before your swing starts. That is easier than fiddling with the swing itself.

Open the face of the club. That gives you more loft than before, but also aligns the clubface to the right of the target. Therefore, you need to compensate by aligning your body, including your shoulders, to the left (**3:18**). Also, move your hands back to a point where they are level with the ball (**3:18a**). These changes will combine to give you a high-flying, soft-landing shot.

Hitting the ball lower also requires some adjustment to your address position.

3:18, 3:18a Simple adjustments to your address position will make it easy for you to play a high, floating lob shot.

3:19, 3:19a, 3:20 Moving the ball towards the back of your stance has the effect of placing your hands forward, with the net result that you de-loft the clubface – ideal for playing a low, punchy shot.

Position the ball back in your stance, but leave your hands opposite the inside of your left thigh (**3:19**). Moving the ball has the effect of shifting your hands forward, so there is no need to overdo it. The net effect is that you deloft the club and produce a steeper angle of attack into the ball. Make a shorter, punchier swing (**3:19a, 3:20**).

Spin shot

This shot should carry a government health warning: it can be damaging to your score. Play it only when you have

3:21 *The heavily flanged sole that is characteristic of the sand wedge makes it unsuitable for tackling shots from hardpan. The pitching wedge is a much safer bet, as its sharper leading edge makes it easy to get under the back of the ball.*

no option as it does not have a high success rate.

Understand, too, that only if you are playing with a balata-covered ball should this shot even be attempted. If you are a devotee of the harder, one-piece ball, forget this shot.

Use a lofted cub. Move the ball back in your stance as you did for the low shot, pick the club up quickly on the backswing and then hit down very sharply. Hit the ball hard. You cannot produce a lot of spin if you hit softly, so you need a shorter backswing and a pronounced acceleration into impact. It is the steepness and abruptness of the downswing that makes this shot so dangerous. You need a very precise contact in order to avoid duffing or thinning the shot. Remember, use it only if your have no other option.

From hardpan

When you have a tight lie, the ball lying on hard, bare ground, use your pitching wedge. Never use your sand wedge. The sand wedge is designed so that the leading edge is higher than the back of the club (3:21). That's perfect for sandplay, but when the ground is hard you run the risk of the club bouncing before it reaches the ball. The result is usually a low, thin shot which flies far past your target.

The pitching wedge, on the other hand, has a lower leading edge. No matter how much you open the face, you can still get the club under the ball.

From a divot

This is not a difficult shot if the ball is in the front of the divot (3:22). When that is the case, you can easily get the club to the back of the ball and play the shot as you would from a normal fairway lie.

The real problem occurs when the ball lies hard against the back of the divot (3:23). You may not even be able to hit the ball at the hole so assess the shot on the basis of the lie. Play the shot you know you can hit, not the one you may be able to bring off once in twenty attempts.

Position the ball back in your stance, as you did to hit the ball lower. That will steepen your downswing sufficiently to get the ball out of the divot and moving forward. Allow for some run on this shot.

want to play the shot, then it probably won't be too difficult. Play it as you would a shot from the fairway. Just allow for a little more run after the ball lands.

If, however, the grass is growing against you, a little more thought is required. You need to make some adjustments. Take no chances. Use a lofted club; the heavy sand wedge is best if the lie is really bad.

Address the shot with your club a little above the grass. That eliminates any possibility of your catching the clubhead in the rough on the way back. Increase your grip pressure. Chances are the grass will grab the clubhead and close the face as you hit the ball, so you need to hold on tight.

3:22, 3:23 When the ball lies at the front of a divot hole you can easily get a club to it, but should it rest against the back of the divot you are only left with one option: play the ball back in your stance and create a fairly steep swing that punches the ball forwards.

From the rough

This is a situation where it is difficult to estimate what kind of contact you are going to get. Long grass has a very abrupt decelerating effect on the club. It is easy to get tangled up and hit the ball nowhere.

Take a good look at your lie (**3:24, 3:24a**). Try to gauge how clean a contact you can make. Determine what is, and what is not, possible. If the grass is growing in the direction in which you

3:24, 3:24a A ball lying in thick rough must be played with as much loft as possible. Don't be greedy in this situation, but take a club that you know will get the ball back into play and strike down and through the shot firmly.

The pitching wedge
RONAN RAFFERTY

The most noticeable difference between a full swing with a driver or medium iron, and a pitch is that as you get closer to the green the body action becomes less involved. Playing a short iron, a shot of, say, 100 yards, the hands and arms assume a more important role as that elusive element of feel is brought to the fore.

Ronan Rafferty illustrates perfectly the distinctive pitch shot swing. Here he faces a shot of some 90 yards, and as you can see, he has made one or two essential adjustments to his set-up position.

First of all you will notice that he stands with his feet a little closer together than normal. As the anticipation is of making a relatively short, three-quarter length swing with a pitching wedge, there is no longer the need for a wide stance, as the body is not required to turn to its fullest extent. Taking a narrow stance immediately places the emphasis on the hands and arms to swing the club, which in this situation is exactly what Ronan is intending.

Furthermore, his stance is slightly open in relation to his target-line, and this helps to give him a good view of the shot that he is about to play. For added clubhead control he has gripped down the shaft an inch or so, and to help guarantee a firm, descending blow, his hands are slightly ahead of the ball.

These adjustments collectively influence the type of swing that Ronan is able to make. The open body position serves to restrict the ability of the body to pivot, and the backswing is made with a combination of arm-swing and shoulder-turn. The hips turn relatively little. At address the weight was spread in favour of the left side, and what transfer of weight there is in the backswing is confined to the legs and knees. It's an instinctive rather than conscious shift onto the right side.

Ronan initiates his downswing with a definite drive forwards with his lower body, and in doing so he creates the space that is necessary for his hands and arms to pull the clubhead down into the ball. Through impact his hands can be seen to pull the clubhead through the ball and as his hands lead the way forwards the follow-through is necessarily quite short.

The ball-turf strike is clearly indicative of a powerful descending attack, and it is this type of swing that creates backspin. The ball is driven forwards, and will land and stop very quickly upon landing on the green.

Playing the high floater

SEVE BALLESTEROS

When you have a receptive green to play at, and a reasonably good lie, floating the ball is a tempting alternative to the standard chip-and-run. It allows you to disregard the slopes and hazards between you and the hole, and so here, for example, Seve is able to fly the ridge that crosses the green and carry the ball virtually all the way to the hole.

Once again, his set-up is the key to pulling this shot off successfully. He plays the ball opposite his left heel, and takes a comfortably narrow stance in which his feet, knees, hips and shoulders are aligned to the left of the flag. You will notice that Seve has his hands slightly behind the ball at address, and that his weight would appear to be favouring his right side. These factors combine to help him get the maximum possible loft from the clubface at impact.

In the backswing Seve basically follows the line of his body, allowing his wrists to hinge naturally in response to the weight of the clubhead as it reaches shoulder height.

Seve is such a tremendous 'feel' player that he can sense the position of the clubhead through his hands, and leaving much of his weight on his right side, he pulls the club back down to the ball – again controlling the position of the clubface instinctively with feel – and slides the blade cleanly beneath the ball. All through the downswing the hips and knees rotate back towards the target, so that by the time the ball is in the air and on its way towards the flag, Seve has completed his follow-through and is facing the line of the shot.

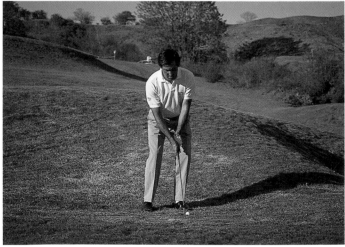

From the Sand

GREENSIDE BUNKERS
by Jim Christine

LONG BUNKER PLAY
by Tim Barter

The most harmful adjective anyone can use to describe a greenside bunker shot is 'explosion'.

A dangerous word that. One mention of it and most players start trying to excavate masses of sand from the bunker. They hit too far behind the ball in the mistaken belief that the more sand they throw onto the green the better the shot will turn out. They are wrong, of course.

The sand wedge, with its wide flange on the bottom of the head, is designed to slide through, not dig into, the sand. This sliding action is the secret to good bunker play.

Set-up

A basic greenside bunker shot is played in much the same way as the pitch described in chapter three. The major difference is

that, for most shots from sand, you must open the face of the club as well as your stance. Only occasionally –when the lip on the trap is relatively insignificant – can you play the shot with the clubface square to the target.

Start by shuffling your feet into the sand. Don't go too deep. Cover the soles of your shoes and no more. That achieves three things: you gain some idea as to the depth and consistency of the sand; it gives you a solid foundation on which to swing; and it lowers the arc of your swing, thereby helping you to hit the sand behind the ball.

Position your hands level with the ball which, in turn, should be opposite your left heel (4:1). Once comfortable, open the face of your club. Do that before you take your grip. If you merely fan the club open after gripping normally, the club will return to square at impact. So the face, although still square to your ball-target line, needs to be open in relation to your stance and body alignment (**4:2**). Recognize, too, that all other variables remaining constant, the ball will fly to the right of your aim. So you must aim left of where you want the

4:1, 4:2 To play a typical greenside bunker shot, you must open the face of the club as well as your stance.

ball to finish. In doing that, open your stance a little more than your shoulders. That will restrict the length of your backswing and make it easier for your downswing to follow your body lines.

The swing

The key here is to keep things simple. Make a normal backswing parallel to your aim. That will guarantee the out-to-in shape, relative to the ball-target line, that you require (**4:3**). There is no need to compound that further by contriving an outside-the-line takeaway; your open stance has already achieved that for you. So don't complicate matters; concentrate instead on making a smooth swing down and through the ball (**4:4, 4:5**).

That word 'through' is important. Your downswing must mirror as closely as possible your backswing. A bunker shot should resemble a regular shot from the fairway. Don't overcomplicate things in your mind. That only causes anxiety and tension, the number one enemies of rhythm and balance in any golf swing.

4:3 A normal backswing parallel to your aim will guarantee the out-to-in swing shape that you require.

4:4, 4:5 Make a smooth swing down and through the ball, splashing the clubface through the sand and popping the ball out in the process.

How much sand?

We've already determined that taking too much sand is not good. But not enough can be just as bad. So how far behind the ball should your club make contact with the sand?

That depends a great deal on the type and consistency of the sand in the bunker. But whatever its texture, the sand does allow you some margin for error. Whether you hit the sand one inch or two inches behind the ball really doesn't make that much difference. The result will be pretty much the same.

I recommend that you aim to strike the sand a couple of inches behind the ball, a measure that is true no matter the length of shot you are playing. Vary the distance the ball travels by varying the length of your backswing. Delicate shots to tightly cut holes don't require a full backswing any more than longer shots require you to make a short backswing.

You do need to make some adjustments when faced with different types of sand. This is especially true when the sand is hard or wet. If you open the face of a sand wedge too much, the flange on the bottom of the club tends to bounce on the hard surface. The leading edge reaches the ball first and the shot is invariably thinned into the face of the bunker or over the green. So play these shots with the clubface closer to square. Use your pitching wedge if you have to. Either aids the sharper leading edge in sliding through the sand under the ball.

Tough situations

In an ideal world, you would never hit your ball into a bunker. And even if you did, it would always be sitting up somewhere in the middle. But you do hit balls into bunkers and they do finish in places where a little experimentation and imagination can come in handy.

That imagination can only take you so far, however. Practise these shots until you are reasonably sure of your capabilities and what to expect. Your basic aim is to recreate your normal address position. You may have to lean forward or back or move the ball around in your stance. But try to put yourself in a position to make what feels like a normal swing. The only way to achieve such an aim is through practise. Never attempt to play a shot you have not practised.

Let's take a look at some of the situations you may encounter.

Plugged ball

This is one occasion when you have to utilize the leading edge of your sand wedge (4:6). Because the ball is below the level of the sand you have to dig to get the ball out. The sharp, leading edge is ideal for the job.

The first thing to do is position the ball back in your stance. In effect, that shifts your hands ahead of the ball. Both encourage the steeper swing path you need in order to get the club to the bottom of the ball.

4:6, 4:7 *When the ball is plugged you must utilize the leading edge of your sand wedge, and adjust your set-up in such a way that you create the steep angle of descent into the sand that is required to get the ball out.*

Next, close the face of your club so that the leading edge is definitely going to reach the sand before the flange. From there, things get easier. Simply hit the sand about an inch behind the ball. Hit hard, almost as hard as you can without throwing yourself at the shot.

Because the club enters the sand on such a steep path, you probably won't be able to follow through very far (**4:7**). The ball will come out lower than normal and run on landing. Backspin is impossible due to the amount of sand between clubface and ball.

Under the lip

Recognising the difficulty of a shot is vital. Sometimes, if the ball is too close to an overhanging lip, the shot is impossible. So don't get carried away by bravado when you are faced with one.

If you feel the ball is playable, the lie of the ball will tell you what kind of shot you are facing. An upslope is not too much of a problem as the ball will automatically fly higher. A flat lie requires some care.

Although you want to open up the face of your sand wedge as much as

4:8, 4:9 When you find your ball under the front lip of a bunker , you must first of all weigh up very carefully the feasiblity of playing a shot forwards. If going forwards is possible, remember that the lip of the bunker will absorb the power of your swing, and will obviously restrict the length of your follow-through.

possible, don't go too far (**4:8**). Remember, the more you open the face, the more the club will bounce. So some adjustment is required.

You must hit the sand closer to the ball than your normally would. The club must bounce under the ball, not before it, if the ball is to fly as high as possible (**4:9**). Obviously, this factor reduces your margin for error, so never try such a shot if you haven't practised it or if you have any doubt as to your prospects of getting the ball out in less than two strokes.

Near the back lip

The first thing to consider here is that you have little chance of getting the ball up quickly. A downhill lie, the sand behind the ball being higher than that in front of it, prevents you from opening the face of the club as much as you would want (**4:10**). If you did open the face and hit the sand behind the ball, the club would bounce too much, resulting in a thinned shot.

So a square to slightly open clubface is best.

As far as your stance is concerned, it is vital that you maintain a 90-degree angle between the slope and your spine so you have to lean forward onto your left foot. That makes it easier for you to swing the club down into the sand (**4:11**). If you leaned back on your right side, the chances are that your club would hit the back lip of the bunker.

When you feel that you are in position, make some practice swings. They will give you a fair idea as to just where the club will make contact with the sand. Suitably reassured, go ahead and make your normal swing.

4:10, 4:11 Playing from a downhill lie near the back-lip of a bunker, it is vital that you maintain a 90-degree angle between the slope and your spine. That makes it easier to swing the club down into the sand and chase the ball forwards .

Ball in, you're not

When the ball is below the level of your feet, you have to use your body in order to get closer to the ball (**4:12**). You have to produce a more upright swing in order to make solid contact. You also need the ball further forward in your stance. That is vital. Think about it. An upright swing is a narrow swing and if you place the ball back in your stance you increase your chances of thinning the shot.

Once you have moved closer to the ball, lean over from your waist. Don't just bend your knees (**4:12a**). If that is all you do to compensate for the position of the ball, your spine angle will still be too vertical and your swing path too flat.

Again, a few practice swings are a good idea. They give you a feel for the shot and quieten any doubt you may have about your unusual address position. When you get it right, swing normally (**4:13, 4:14, 4:14a**).

4:12, 4:12a
Whenever the ball is below the level of your feet, you must mould your body into position to compensate, and the key is to bend over from the waist, not the knees.

4:13, 4:14, 4:14a *Once you are comfortable, make a normal swing, but remember to keep your head still until the ball is up and on its way.*

LONG BUNKER PLAY
by Tim Barter

The most important part of any long bunker shot is the preparation and thought that precedes its execution. In fact, your appraisal of any potentially hazardous situation is crucial. This is a time to be totally realistic with yourself, and about your capabilities.

Your first consideration must always be the lie of the ball. That alone will determine the feasability of playing any shot from a bunker. Examine the ball and its position in the sand before you go any further. If distance is your aim, then you must ascertain whether or not it is possible to make a clean enough contact with the ball to carry it to safety. If the lie is prohibitive, then your hopes of a spectacular recovery are dashed. You must accept the fact that you have found a hazard, and play accordingly. The only sensible solution then is to plan an escape that will put you back into play with the minimum amount of risk.

The severity of the front lip of the bunker, and your proximity to it, are two further influences on your strategy from sand. Obviously your main objective must be to get the ball out of the bunker and back into play. You must therefore take a club that has sufficient loft to lift the ball over the front lip.

Again you must be totally realistic about this. Don't take the club that you need to cover the distance to the target if it does not have the loft necessary to get the ball up and out of the bunker. All you will succeed in doing is driving the ball into the face of the bunker and into a much worse position. Take the club that you know will get you out, one that will allow you to play a shot with full confidence (**4:15**).

If the ball is submerged in the sand, and the front lip of the bunker prevents you making any significant forward progress, then take your sand wedge and simply play to that part of the fairway that offers you the best shot into the

4:15 Whenever you are in the sand your first objective is simply to get out, and to do that you must always take a club that has sufficient loft to clear the front lip.

green. Playing your next shot from the fairway is far better than leaving the ball in the sand.

Assuming that lie and lip are in your favour, the technique for playing a fairway bunker shot varies relatively little from that of a shot from the fairway. The most obvious difference is that, in the sand, your footing is likely to be less stable. This will, to a certain extent, depend upon the texture of the sand itself, but generally speaking, you will need to take special care when adopting your stance. In order to improve your stability, shuffle your feet down into the sand a little. This helps you to establish a good foundation from which to swing. Doing

this will also indicate to you the texture of the sand. Valuable information can be learned through the feet.

Having shuffled your feet down into the sand until you feel confident enough to make a swing, you must then compensate for the fact you have actually lowered your body in relation to the ball, and to do this you should grip the club a little way down the shaft (**4:16**). As a general rule, go down the shaft as far as you have shuffled your feet into the sand. Shortening the effective length of the club in this way will also serve to increase your control over the clubhead.

These shots should be played with limited footwork to avoid putting unnecessary pressure on your potentially vulnerable stance. This will have the effect of limiting your hip turn and shortening your swing slightly. If conditions allow, take one more club than the distance would normally dictate, and employ an easy, three-quarter length swing. Good long bunker technique relies more heavily on a co-ordinated hand and arm action. Maintaining a good tempo is vital. Don't be intimidated by the fact that you are in sand, and let your rhythm desert you. If you swing too vigorously you will only succeed in losing your

4:16 Having shuffled your feet down into the sand for stability, compensate for the fact that you have actually lowered your body in relation to the ball by simply gripping the club a little way down the shaft.

footing and this will cause you to make contact with the sand before the ball.

Let's look at the basic shots of long bunker play.

80-yard wedge

The set-up for this shot is virtually as it would be for a pitch of a similar distance from the fairway (4:17). Providing that you have a good, clean lie, the only adjustments that you will need to make are those that will help you maintain your stability during the stroke, enabling you to strike the ball as cleanly as possible. Think about the strike that you intend to make. With long shots out of bunkers the ball must be hit before the sand. Hitting the sand before the ball would have the same deadening effect as hitting the ground before the ball when playing from the fairway.

First, you must build a sound foundation for your body. Shuffle your feet into the sand and, once you are comfortable, compensate for the fact that you have lowered your height in relation to the ball by gripping down the club by a corresponding amount. Then think about your ball position. Your intention is to strike the ball cleanly with a slightly descending blow before the clubhead lightly brushes the sand. Playing the ball from the middle of your stance is ideal (4.18). That will enable your hands to

4:17, 4:18 Shuffle your feet into the sand and build a sound foundation upon which to swing. For the purposes of striking the ball cleanly before the clubhead meets the sand, position the ball towards the middle of your stance.

fall comfortably into position, being slightly ahead of the ball and just opposite the inside of your left thigh. Settle your weight down into the sand, and feel that it slightly favours your left side. That will help to encourage a relatively steep swing and a descending strike on the back of the ball. Flex your knees firmly so that they offer your upper body a totally effective suspension unit.

Your body alignment is important. I believe that you should aim to play this type of shot with just a suspicion of cutspin, as that will help you to pick the ball cleanly from the sand. In order to create a slight cutting action across the ball through impact, align your body fractionally to the left of the ball-target line. The position of your body will determine the line that your swing should follow. The clubface, however, should be square to the target line, and it is as a result of this clubface position and slightly out-to-in clubhead path that cutspin is created.

Down the line you can see quite clearly the extent to which the backswing is restricted. Aim to make as full a shoulder turn as your restricted lower body action will allow (**4:19, 4:19a**). In fact, to ensure that your legs do contain the swing comfortably, concentrate on keeping your footwork to a minimum in the backswing. Remember, this is a swing

4:19, 4:19a Aim to make as full a shoulder-turn as your restricted lower-body action will allow. Remember that this is a swing that is controlled predominantly by the shoulders, hands and arms.

that is controlled predominantly by the shoulders, hands and arms. Your body should be free to support and respond to your swinging arms.

In the downswing, your thoughts should be directed only towards the contact that you intend to make with the ball. Always focus on the part of the ball that you intend to hit, and not on

the sand (**4:20**). Clear your weight to the left through impact and finish with your swing in perfect balance and under control (**4:21**).

Assuming that you do make a clean contact, the distance that you will hit the ball is controlled by the length of the backswing that you make. A full 80-yard shot like this requires that

4:20, 4:21 As you start your downswing, focus on the part of the ball that you intend to hit, and not on the sand. Clear your weight through impact and finish with your body in balance.

you make a relatively full backswing while a 60-yard shot would require a slightly shorter backswing. Only practise will help you to establish your own range.

Playing a long iron

When you face a bunker shot of some considerable distance, the elements of lie and lip become all the more important. Playing a long iron demands a perfect lie, and that the front lip of the bunker is virtually negligible. Only if you are fortunate enough to find your ball in such an advantageous position can you safely play for distance (**4:22**).

Before you make any attempt to play, give some thought to your club selection. If, in normal circumstances, you would use a 5-iron for a shot of, say, 160 yards, then drop back to a 4-iron in the bunker. That will allow you to choke down on the club and swing easily, but yet still give you sufficient distance. Again, make the necessary adjustments to your stance by shuffling your feet into the sand.

The main difference between playing a long iron, a medium iron or a pitching wedge from the sand – and this corresponds with the difference that you would expect if you were playing similar shots from the fairway – is that the ball must be positioned progressively further forward in your stance (**4:23, 4:23a**). In chapter one the ball position was referred to as being accommodated within a three-ball span, and this holds true from the

4:22, 4:23, 4:23a
Playing a long iron from a fairway bunker is only feasible when the ball is lying perfectly and the lip of the bunker is virtually negligible.

4:24, 4:24a When distance is your goal, focus on the top of the ball and concentrate on making a compact, three-quarter length backswing.

sand. To promote a clean sweeping action through impact with the longer irons, the ball should be placed more towards your front foot, so that it is struck as the clubhead shallows out at the lowest point in its arc .

When distance is your goal, a clean contact is essential. Focusing on the top of the ball and firming up your grip pressure a little will help to encourage this. The swing itself is then simply a compact, three-quarter length action (**4:24, 4:24a**). Concentrate on a smooth tempo and on maintaining your height through impact. This will ensure that the ball is swept cleanly from the sand (**4:25**).

4:25, 4:26 In the downswing, concentrate on maintaining a good rhythm, and sweep the ball cleanly from the sand. Despite the uncertainty of footwork in the sand, your follow-through position should reflect the control with which you have executed the stroke.

A well balanced follow-through position should reflect the control with which you have executed the stroke (**4:26**).

As you can see, I have aimed towards the right hand side of the green. There are two reasons for this. Firstly, the natural lie of the land ahead will gather the ball to the left, but more importantly I am guarding against finding further trouble directly in front of the bunker and around the green should I fail to make a perfect contact. Remember that your assessment of the potential dangers that surround this shot is as important as the stroke itself. You must be decisive. If you doubt your ability to

4:27, 4:27a With an exceptionally good lie, it is possible to play a fairway wood from a bunker. The 5-wood, with its small head, is ideal.

get the ball up and out of the bunker with the club that you have chosen, then think again. From where would you most like to play your next shot? Think about all the possible outcomes, and play the shot which is most likely to be successful.

Playing a fairway wood

With an exceptionally good lie – and when the front lip is virtually non-existent – it is sometimes possible to play a fairway wood from a bunker (**4.27, 4.27a**). With its small head, a 5-wood is

ideal. Make the same adjustments as you did to play a long iron, but this time position the ball further forward in your stance, to the point where it is opposite the inside of your left heel. Shuffle your feet in the sand and grip down the shaft for added clubhead control. Again, there will be relatively little lower body action (**4.28**). The swing relies on a good hand, arm and upper body movement and requires immaculate rhythm and timing in order to achieve a clean sweep through impact (**4.29**).

4:28, 4:29 A full swing like this relies on good hand, arm and upper body co-ordination, and will also require immaculate rhythm and timing in order to sweep the ball away cleanly.

Blasting the ball forwards

Each of the examples so far have featured a perfect lie, but out on the course, you may not always be so lucky. There will be times when playing for distance is out of the question, and then you must consider your options very carefully and make the best out of a bad situation.

If the ball is totally plugged and the face of the bunker is quite severe, then you must reach for your sand wedge and simply blast it out to safety, probably sideways. But if the ball is only part-submerged, and the front lip does not present too much of a problem, it is possible to play a chasing shot that will move the ball a considerable distance up the fairway.

To do this you need to create a swing that produces a steep angle of attack, so that the ball – and with it a fairly large chunk of sand – is driven forwards.

It is possible to build the necessary ingredients for success for this shot into your address position (**4:30, 4:30a**). Take an 8- or 9-iron, and place the ball back in your stance. At the same time, shift the majority of your weight onto your left side and make sure that your hands are ahead of the ball, tilting the clubshaft towards your target. The clubface should be square to your intended line.

This 'weight left, ball back' combination will induce the steeper swing arc that this shot requires without you having to think about it. All you need to do is make a good arm swing and drive the clubhead through the sand, so that the ball is squeezed forwards (**4:31**). You should aim to make contact with the sand about half an inch behind the ball, and

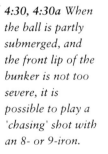

4:30, 4:30a When the ball is partly submerged, and the front lip of the bunker is not too severe, it is possible to play a 'chasing' shot with an 8- or 9-iron.

4:31, 4:32 *A good arm swing, with your weight favouring your left side, will drive the clubhead through the sand, squeezing the ball forwards with a chunk of sand. Don't be intimidated by the lie; trust your swing and be forceful!*

then chase the clubhead forward in the follow-through (**4:32**). Don't be intimidated by the lie. Make the necessary adjustments, trust your swing and be forceful.

Ball above or below your feet

Whenever the ball is above or below the level of your feet – and this applies universally, whether you are in a bunker or not – it is vital that you make allowances for this discrepancy at address, and not with a series of compensatory moves during the swing itself. Your address position must be flexible enough to negotiate any given situation.

If the ball is above your feet, then

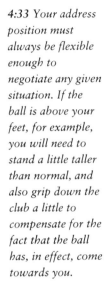

4:33 Your address position must always be flexible enough to negotiate any given situation. If the ball is above your feet, for example, you will need to stand a little taller than normal, and also grip down the club a little to compensate for the fact that the ball has, in effect, come towards you.

you must make certain adjustments to accommodate it within a comfortable set-up position. In effect, the ball has come towards you, and so you will need to stand up a little taller than usual (**4:33**). Your spine angle will be forced up slightly, and you will need to grip the club a little further down the shaft to assist you to hit the ball cleanly. Aim a little to the right of your intended target, as the ball will move from right-to-left through the air. Then you should swing smoothly, and concentrate on maintaining your balance.

If the ball is below the level of your feet, the opposite adjustments must be made. First, you will need to aim to the left of your target to allow for the inevitable left-to-right deviation of the ball through the air. You should also utilize the full length of the clubshaft, so grip it normally, just below the butt end. Depending on just how far the ball is below the level of your feet, you will also need to increase your spine angle in order to position the clubhead behind the ball (**4:34**). To do this you should bend over from the hips. It is important that you maintain the spinal angle you create at address throughout your swing. If you should straighten your body, you will effectively lift the club up and either top the ball or miss it altogether. Ensure that you are in a stable position before you attempt to swing and feel that your weight is spread evenly between your feet. A couple of practice backswings will help

to familiarize you with the feeling of making the slightly more upright swing that this address position will create. As your stability is obviously going to be extremely vulnerable, you must certainly never try to hit the ball too hard.

4:34 Whenever the ball is below the level of your feet, you will naturally be forced to increase your spine angle, and to do that you should bend over from the hips.

The basic splash shot

NICK FALDO

The object of the splash shot is to deliver the clubface into the sand a couple of inches behind the ball and continue through to remove a shallow divot of sand which has the effect of throwing the ball up and towards the target. The set-up is geared totally towards the action, and the first thing that you will notice about Nick Faldo's address position is just how open his stance is in relation to the target. His feet, knees, hips and shoulders are all aligned to the left of the flag, and that's exactly the line that his swing is now programmed to follow. Provided that he does so, he will produce the shallow 'U'-shaped swingpath that characterizes a good bunker shot.

To compensate for his open body position, the clubface is also open at address, thus aiming at the flag. The ball is positioned just opposite the inside of Nick's left instep, and his weight is spread evenly, although if anything it should favour his left side.

The low positioning of his hands at address encourages Nick to hinge his wrists early on in the backswing, and this is a position that he then maintains all the way to the top of his backswing. The club is set in the perfect position at the top, and he is ready to drive forwards and accelerate the club through the sand beneath the ball in the downswing.

As you would expect from a player of Faldo's quality, tempo plays an enormous part in producing a good bunker shot. His change in direction is effortless, and having set the club in a perfect position at the top of his backswing, he simply accelerates the clubhead down into the sand beneath the ball. He maintains his balance and continues to extend the clubhead forwards through the sand to a full finish.

One way in which you can improve your own tempo is to concentrate on making your follow-through the same length as your backswing, just as Faldo does. That will help you to keep the club moving smoothly and effortlessly through the sand. Obviously, when you are in sand, your footing is often less secure than it would be on grass, and so your leg action is inevitably limited. As a result, the swing is controlled predominantly by the hands, arms and shoulders, and as Faldo demonstrates beautifully here, it should be executed with poise and balance.

The only way to become truly familiar with the distance that you hit the ball from sand is to practise. Don't be afraid to vary the length of your swing and the amount of sand that you take. As with any shot – but particularly the short shots which involve a great deal of touch – regular practice is essential if you want to produce bunker shots of quality.

Shaping Shots
by John Stirling

If you go to watch a professional golf tournament or a top-class amateur event, you will witness at first hand the great ability that the top players have to manoeuvre the ball through the air at will. This ability to shape shots is the hallmark of a truly good player. Someone who not only has the vision but the ability to fashion a stroke into a green or to match the shape of the fairway from the tee. This is the art of shotmaking; manufacturing shots to counteract the natural lie of the land; to defeat the wind or to simply attack a pin that is tucked away behind a bunker. With a variety of shots possible, the player who can move the ball through the air opens up a lot of otherwise inaccessable scoring opportunities.

There's another useful benefit, too. The player who can produce a shape of shot to order will find that the target is effectively enlarged. If a fairway is 40 yards wide and the player, let's say for example, Lee Trevino, is most comfortable playing a controlled fade, then he has the whole width of the fairway in which to land the ball (**5:1**). Aiming down the left hand margin, a player like Trevino can let the ball drift back into the heart of the fairway. The late Bobby Locke, the great South African player who won four Open Championships, preferred to play a natural draw, and so he could aim down the right hand side of the fairway and watch as the ball soared from right-to-left back into safety. Ian Woosnam is another who favours the draw and it is wonderful to watch him unleash a drive with such confidence knowing that the ball will return with a right-to-left shape (**5:2**). So you see, the actual target for the player who can be sure of manoeuvring the ball through the air is, in fact, twice as wide as that of the player who aims to bisect the fairway.

Of course, every player has a

5:1 Lee Trevino has always relied on the fade, and he starts the ball well to the left of his intended target, safe in the knowledge that it will float gently back onto line.

5:2 Ian Woosnam, on the other hand, is a good example of a player who plays with a natural draw, and he can confidently fire the ball down the right hand side of the fairway and watch as it turns back to the left.

favourite way of moving the ball, whether it is from right-to-left or from left-to-right. And it makes good sense to cultivate the shot that comes naturally to you. Always play to your strengths. Much will depend on your grip, and so once again we are reminded of the ever present consequence of the fundamentals. As I mentioned in the opening chapter, the way in which you hold the club has a direct effect on the position of the clubface at impact, and so your grip inevitably influences the shape of every single shot that you hit. The player who holds the club with a hooker's grip will, as you would rightly assume, tend to play with a right-to-left shape.

Bernhard Langer is just such a player. He has a very strong hooker's grip, with his left hand turned noticeably to the right on the club at address (**5:3**). While it is generally considered normal to see the first two knuckles on the back of the left hand, Langer displays between

5:3, 5:4 Bernhard Langer plays with a strong left hand grip, displaying between three and four knuckles on that hand at address, a fault that would normally be expected to produce a severe hook. But such is Langer's talent that he offsets his fault with an early release of his lower body, and plays with a controlled draw.

5:5, 5:6 Nick Faldo, who is altogether more orthodox, and plays with a neutral grip, is more inclined to flight the ball from left-to-right, a shot that he can produce to order, as he did at the 15th hole at Wentworth in the 1989 World Matchplay Final (below), setting up a most unexpected birdie-3.

three and four knuckles. This would normally lead to the player closing the clubface on the ball at impact, producing a severe hook, but such is Langer's talent that he is able to offset his 'fault' with a fast unwinding of his lower body through impact, and play with a controlled draw (5:4).

The player who favours a neutral grip will be more inclined to be able to play with a slight left-to-right fade (5:5). Nick Faldo provides a classic example. The relationship that he creates between his hands and the clubface at address is

perfectly maintained throughout his swing. You may well remember Faldo's glorious 3-iron shot from beneath the trees on the right hand side of the 15th fairway at Wentworth during the PGA Championship in 1989 (**5:6**). With no direct route to the green open, Faldo played the most controlled fade around the trees that finished just a few feet from the pin. It was a shot of sheer precision, and the resulting birdie helped Faldo to victory.

The majority of professionals and low handicap players generally play with a natural draw. They strike the ball as the club is moving along the correct inside-to-square-to-inside path, and produce a powerful, penetrating right-to-left flight. But they could produce a fade on request. That's the crux of the matter. The truly good player not only understands the special technique that shaping shots involves, but he has the ability to move the ball either way, and at any given time. That's why the late Sir Henry Cotton won three Open Championships. He had the most wonderful clubface control, and he could play a host of different shots from every lie imaginable. Hours and hours of practice had rewarded him with absolute control of the golf ball. At the highest level in the game it is that degree of control that separates the good from the great.

Seve Ballesteros is another magician with the golf club (**5:7**). Not only does he have an inspired imagination, but dedicated practice has taught him how to control the clubface. To watch Seve cut up a softly landing lob shot with a 2-iron, or flight a driver so delicately that it lands and holds a green

5:7 Seve Ballesteros can play a fade or a draw to order such is the degree of control he has over the clubhead.

no more than 150 yards away is to fully appreciate the skill of a world-class player.

If I was a young player with hopes and aspirations of becoming a real champion, I would be practising all the shots, and not just the ones that came easily to me. Of course you will have a favourite shape of shot, and that's the one that must form the basis of your golf game, the one that's natural. But strive to develop your repertoire.

Clubhead path and clubface position

Shaping the ball requires first that you gather an understanding of the clubhead path and how the position of the clubface at impact in relation to that path affects the flight of the ball. Such understanding – and ultimately control – comes only with hard practice.

In the opening chapter I stressed the importance of the set-up position, and explained that it is your set-up that determines the shape and direction of your swing and the shape of the shot. What you are trying to achieve at address is a preview of your body and clubface position at impact. Think of your address and impact positions as being virtually the same thing. In reality, of course, impact is a position that is reached at great speed, and as your body is responding quite naturally to the athletic movement of your swing, there are bound to be a few subtle differences. But so far as your hands and the clubface are concerned,

they will return to the same position at impact as they were originally placed at address.

Normally the set-up is designed to position your body and the clubface in parallel harmony, the grip serving as the essential coupling unit between you and the club. Deliberately producing a fade or a draw requires that you offset the position of the clubface in relation to your body at address. Simply stated, you must aim the clubface at the spot where you want the ball to end up, and then align your body – and thus the direction of your swing – along the path on which you want the ball to start. Always set the clubface first, then position your body. Your swing path will automatically produce the correct starting flight of the ball, while your clubface position will induce the curvature that you need. To play a fade you must create the situation in which the body is open to your clubface and the line of your swing through impact. For the draw, the body must be closed in relation to your clubface and your swing as it meets the ball. I believe that this method represents the easiest and most reliable way to shape the flight of the ball. A simple adjustment in your address position will effect these necessary changes for you.

Before we look in more detail at the mechanics involved with shaping the ball, let me stress the importance of practice. To become proficient in the art of shotmaking you will need to spend a considerable amount of time simply hitting balls and getting used to the feeling of swinging across your target line. Take square, open and closed stances. Play the ball well forward in your stance, well back and everywhere in between. Experiment with your swing plane and find out just what effect your hands can have on the flight of the ball. There are endless combinations. As you prepare to make each shot, picture in your mind your intended ball flight to the target and feel the motion and flow of the swing that will send the ball there.

Playing the fade

The fade is generally considered to be a much safer shot than a draw. The high-flying, left-to-right shape is ideal for attacking a pin that is tucked away in the corner of a green, or for simply stopping the ball quickly within a limited landing area. Ideally the draw would be the shape that you would want to play with the woods and long irons, producing the low, penetrating flight that achieves the maximum distance. The majority of professionals tend to favour the draw for their long shots, but then often substitute the softer fade for their approach shots to the green. It's really a matter of preference. Versatility is the key.

Let's assume that you were playing a long iron shot, say a 4-iron, to a green at a distance of 170 yards away (5:8).

5:8 When you set up to play a fade, imagine a tennis player executing a firmly struck cross-court slice. The hand action that he uses through impact is very similar to that which the golfer employs, pulling the clubface across the ball and spinning it from left-to-right.

The flag is tucked away to the right hand side of the green, and so the perfect shot is a fade.

First, you must set the clubface aiming just to the left of the flag (5:9). Then, make an orthodox grip but set your feet, knees, hips and shoulders left of the parallel line to the target (5:10). Grip a

5:9 To create the imbalance that is necessary to play the fade, first aim the clubface normally at your target.

5:10, 5:11 Then, make an orthodox grip but align your feet, knees, hips and shoulders to the left of your target line. These adjustments to your se up will produce the out-to-in attack on the ball that you desire, and as lo as you concentrate on swinging the club along the line of your body the clubshaft should parallel the line across your toes at the top of your backswing.

little more firmly than normal with your left hand and a little more lightly with your right. This will encourage your left hand to lead the clubhead into the ball, while reducing the tendency for your right hand to roll the clubface closed at impact. As long as you trust your set-up and swing accordingly, these slight

5:12, 5:13 Through impact you should have a definite feeling of unwinding your body ahead of the clubhead. As long as you do that, and lead the clubhead through the ball with your hands, you will produce the left-to-right spin that you desire.

5:14 Suppressing the release of the clubhead in this way, the follow-through is naturally restricted as the right hand is not encouraged to cross over the left.

adjustments at address will produce a shot that starts to the left of the target before gently curving back onto it. This open body position will produce a slightly out-to-in attack on the ball, and that's what produces the fade.

Your set-up is the key. Once you are in position, keep your hands passive and swing the club along the line of your body. At the top of your backswing the clubshaft should parallel the line across your toes, and point to the left of your target (**5:11**). The clubface itself should be in a perfectly neutral position, in line with the back of your left hand. Check your backswing position in a mirror.

Through impact the feeling that you should have is very much one of unwinding your body ahead of the clubhead (**5:12**). Playing the fade, there should be a definite feeling of lateness through the ball, a feeling of holding the blade off as long as possible before pulling your left hand through the shot (**5:13**). In doing this you are effectively guaranteeing a shot that cannot possibly go left. As long as you lead the clubhead with your hands through the ball you will produce left-to-right spin. At impact your body should be open relative to the clubface, and the clubface itself should be travelling across the ball as opposed to through it. The back of your left hand should lead the clubhead through the impact area. There should be no rollover whatsoever, and consequently your follow-through will be somewhat

restricted (**5:14**). You are suppressing the club rather than releasing it.

In many ways the fade is a defensive stroke, and as the ball flies a little higher than normal you will find that you do lose a little distance. When

5:15 The opposite adjustments are made to play a draw. First, align the clubface squarely towards your intended target.

5:16 Then, position your body so that your feet, knees hips and shoulders are aligned to the right of the line on which you intend the ball to start.

you play a fade take at least one extra club, and always swing smoothly.

Playing the draw

Creating the necessary imbalance between your body and clubface alignment that spins the ball from right-to-left involves following just the opposite procedure to that which we designed for the fade. Align the clubface squarely to your target (**5:15**), but this time set your feet, knees, hips and shoulders aiming to the right of the line on which you intend the ball to start (**5:16**). When you set up to play a draw, make sure that the clubface is closed in relation to the direction of your swing. The more spin that you wish to impart, the further right you should aim your body and the more the clubface should be closed in relation to it.

Once you have incorporated these alterations into your set-up position, your swing should again be relatively straight forward. Simply follow the line of your body (**5:17**). At the top of your backswing the club should point to the right of your target (**5:18**), and here you will be in the perfect position to attack the ball powerfully from the inside. Through impact there should be a definite feeling

5:17 The tennis player analogy is again applicable for the draw. This time, as you prepare to play, picture in your mind a tennis player firing a powerful forehand topspin pass. Again the hand action through impact is similar to that of the golfer spinning the ball from right-to-left, featuring a definite roll of the right wrist through impact and so closing the clubface on the ball.

5:18 Provided that you trust your set-up, and swing along the line of your body, the clubshaft will now point to the right of your target at the top of your backswing.

5:19 Through impact there should be a definite feeling of releasing the clubhead freely, rolling your wrists and following the line of the shot with your right hand.

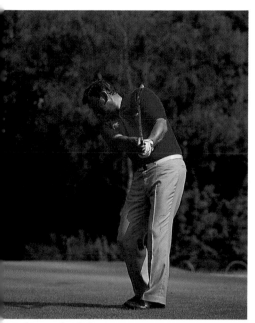

*20 Playing the fade, your hand
*tion is restricted, but when you play
*draw it is essential that your right
*nd is allowed to overtake the left
ough impact.

*:21 The momentum of the club should be
*ufficient to carry you all the way to a full
ollow-through position.

of releasing the clubhead freely, rolling
the wrists and following the line of the
shot with your right hand (**5:19**). It may
help if you think of this action as being
similar to that of an uninhibited forehand
tennis stroke, allowing the right hand to
cross over the left and so closing the
clubface on the ball. Playing the fade,
there should be no crossover of the hands
whatsoever, but when you play a draw it
is essential that your right hand is allowed
to smoothly overtake the left through
impact (**5:20**). Make a full swing, and let
the momentum of the club carry you all
the way to a proud, tall follow-through
position (**5:21**).

Shaping your shots from the tee

Often you will find that a hole is designed
to be played with a certain shape of shot
from the tee. If a hole features a dog-leg,
either from left-to-right or right-to-left,
then shaping your tee shot will often yield
a worthwhile reward. If a hole is guarded
on either flank by trees or some other
potentially threatening hazard, then
shaping a shot away from that trouble is
another safety measure that can prove to
be valuable. It is essential that you make
a thorough appraisal of the situation
before deciding on the shot to play.

Whenever you are considering
playing either a fade or a draw from the
tee, remember that it is much easier to
fade a straight-faced club and draw a
more lofted club. When you seek a fade,

and when distance is a factor, take your driver or 1-iron and tee the ball a little lower than you would usually. This will serve to consciously steepen the plane of your swing and will also ensure that you strike the middle of the ball. These factors

destination of the ball, make your grip, and then adopt an open body position in relation to your target, with the ball placed slightly further forward than normal (**5:22**). Trust your set-up and swing accordingly. At the top of your

5:22, 5:23 When you seek to play a fade from the tee, remember that it is much easier to fade a straight-faced club. Take your driver or 1-iron and tee the ball a little lower than normal. Then programme your swing adjustments at address: aim the clubface at your intended target but adopt an open body position in relation to that target. Trust your set-up and swing normally.

combined will help you to impart the necessary left-to-right sidespin.

The adjustments that you make at address will again predetermine the shape of your swing. In anticipation of a fade, aim the clubface at the intended final

backswing the clubshaft should correspond with the line across your feet, which means that it will point to the left of your target (**5:23**). This is purely evidence that your swing has followed the line of your body. The discrepancy between your clubface alignment and your swing path will produce the fade that you require.

Alternatively, if you encounter a situation that calls for a pronounced draw, then select your 3-wood from the withstand being fractionally closed at impact. Tee the ball a little higher than normal, aim the clubface at your intended target and then align your body to the right of your target line (**5:24**). Grip the club lightly and make a free, uninhibited

5:24, 5:25 You will need to make the opposite adjustments to play a draw, but remember that when your aim is to close the clubface on the ball at impact, you effectively subtract loft, and so you will need to take a more lofted club than normal. From the tee, for example, take your 3-wood and not your driver.

tee and not your driver. When you play a draw you effectively subtract loft from the clubface, and if you take your driver, a club which has hardly any loft at all to begin with, there will be nothing left at impact. Your 3-wood has sufficient loft to swing, again following the line of your body (**5:25**). The powerful inside attack that you create will produce a low draw as long as you release the clubhead through impact and follow the flight of the ball with your right hand.

Now let's look at how you can fashion shots to defeat the wind.

Playing the low ball

There are few more testing examinations for the golfer than playing directly into a strong wind. Any slight mis-hit is greatly exaggerated. Into the wind, if you strike the ball with the slightest hint of a draw or fade, it is quickly blown into a severe hook or slice. Your margin for error is therefore reduced to such a degree that the only viable solution is to play a knockdown shot low beneath the teeth of the wind.

When you hear a player describe a shot as being played 'under the wind', he is describing a low shot that is played with a three-quarter swing, and with two or three clubs more than the actual distance would usually dictate. The secret is to swing as smoothly and easily as possible. To play a low shot you must first set about decreasing the effective loft that you offer to the back of the ball. The easiest way to do this is to move the ball back in your stance (**5:26**). This will automatically place your hands ahead of the clubhead and effectively de-loft the clubface. For added control, grip the club a little shorter than normal. The key to playing these shots successfully is to reproduce this position at impact, chasing the ball forwards with a low, penetrating flight.

It is important that you play a low shot without too much wrist action. Aim to make a fairly low, restricted backswing and a similarly short follow-through (**5:27**). Keep your weight left, and lead the clubhead with your hands. In other words, seek to create a punching action

5:26 To play a low shot you must first set about decreasing the effective loft on the clubface, and the easiest way to do that is move the ball back in your stance.

5:27 The low shot is played with relatively little wrist action: aim to make a fairly low, restricted backswing, and a similarly short, punchy follow-through.

5:28 To play the high ball you want to get as much loft as possible on the clubface at impact, and the most logical way of achieving this is to place the ball forwards in your stance.

5:29, 5:30 Feel that your weight falls primarily onto your right side – as it would were you about to throw a ball high into the air – and picture a high finish to your swing.

through impact, driving the ball forwards rather than upwards. If you incorporate too much wrist action and swing too hard you increase the chances of imparting the backspin which sends the ball upwards. Hand action creates height. A wristy pitch, for example, will fly much higher than a firm wristed chip shot. In practice, we are simply extending this principle in the long game, and playing the low ball with a firm-wristed, shallow swing.

Playing the high ball

To get the ball up high the opposite adjustments must obviously apply. You need as much loft as possible on the clubface at impact, and the most logical way of achieving this is to place the ball well forwards in your stance (**5:28**). This will automatically bring your hands back to a position level with the clubhead. Your grip should be relatively light to encourage greater use of your hands during the stroke. Feel is important. Sense the clubhead on the end of the shaft and feel that you pick the club up relatively quickly on the backswing and deliver it smartly back to the ball with plenty of hand action. Imagine you were preparing to throw a ball high into the air (**5:29**). In anticipation of the throw the right side of your body would fall naturally under the left. Think about this as you set up to hit a high shot. Feel that your weight falls primarily onto your right side, and picture a high finish to your swing (**5:30**).

To summarize, play your high shots with the ball forward in your stance

5:31 The easiest way to deal with a crosswind is to simply play to the conditions. For example, if the wind is blowing across the hole from the right, then aim to the right to compensate for the fact that the flight of your ball is going to be affected. Similarly, if the wind is blowing from the left, aim further left and let your ball sail back in the wind.

and your hands back, and for low shots move the ball back with your hands forward.

Playing through a crosswind

Playing through a crosswind offers a classic opportunity for clubhead and ball control. The better player should feel the clubhead, and manipulate his hand action through the ball to impart a compensatory spin. For example, if the wind is blowing across your line from right-to-left, firm up your grip in the left hand and pull through the shot firmly with that hand (5:31). This will have the effect of introducing the heel of the club to the ball first, producing a left-to-right spin which combats the right-to-left wind.

Into a left-to-right wind, gripping more tightly with your right hand would have the opposite effect. If you associate your right hand with the toe end of the club you will find that hitting harder with the right hand produces a slightly closed clubface through impact which imparts right-to-left spin. This will hold the ball against a left-to-right wind and help to produce a relatively straight shot.

Alternatively, you can combat a crosswind simply by allowing for the

strength of the wind when you set up to the ball. Aim to the left of your target when the wind is blowing from left-to-right, and aim to the right of your target when the wind is blowing across your line from right-to-left.

Playing from an uphill/downhill lie

Whenever you are faced with an awkward lie, the key to success rests with your ability to adopt a compensatory set-up position. What you must attempt to achieve is a body position which sets the spine at right angles to the slope of the ground. In other words, you must strive to duplicate the position that you would adopt for a normal shot from level ground.

Your stability during any stroke is a most important factor. If you lose balance you lose control. At address you must make the compensations necessary to transfer part of your body weight into the slope while at the same time retaining the ideal body position. Then you will be able to swing normally and maintain balance. Your hips, legs and knees should provide the support, leaving your upper body free to swing easily. As a general rule you should play the ball more towards the higher foot and let your weight follow the slope.

Facing an uphill lie your left leg will need to be flexed a little more than the right, and you should position the ball towards your higher foot, in this case the

5:32, 5:32a
Playing any shot from an upslope (above) will effectively add loft to whichever club you are using. Note the difference in loft to a shot played from a straight lie (left). Always take this into account when pondering your club selection.

111

left foot. Create the necessary angles in your knees, and settle your weight firmly on the balls of your feet. Playing the ball forwards in your stance from an upslope will effectively increase the loft on the clubface at impact, and you can expect shots from this position to fly a little higher than normal (**5:32, 5:32a**). For that reason it will be necessary to select at least one, possibly two, clubs more than the distance would usually dictate.

5:33 When the slope runs away from you, the opposite is true. A downhill lie effectively delofts the clubface, and so you must be prepared for a shot that flies lower than normal.

When the slope runs away from you, it is your right leg that must be flexed in order that you maintain a stable position with your spine at right angles to the slope. In this position the majority of your weight should be supported by your left leg.

Play the ball towards your higher foot, this time the right foot, and remember that a downhill lie effectively delofts the clubface at impact, so in principle always take less club on such shots (**5:33**).

Playing with the ball above/below your feet

Whenever the ball is above or below your feet, your aim must be to negate the effect of the slope as much as possible. If the ball is below the level of your stance then you must avoid the normal reaction of simply bending over from the waist. You must retain your normal address posture, and the only way that you can do that and at the same time get the club beneath the ball is to flex your knees more than usual, as far as is necessary to rest the club comfortably behind the ball. The slope forces you to make an exaggeratedly upright swing, and invariably these shots will tend to fade away to the right during their flight. Make provision for this by aiming your body to the left edge of your target (**5:34**).

In the reverse situation, when the ball is considerably above the level of your feet, you must make the necessary adjustments to avoid striking the ground before the ball. The way to do this is to first of all choke down on the grip. Then adjust the flex in your knees to correspond with the position of the ball. You will need to stand up a little straighter, but make sure that you at least retain that feeling of athleticism in your stance. Your stance may need to be a little wider than normal to assist in keeping proper balance. When the clubface is placed behind a ball that is higher than the level of your feet it will tend to face to the left of your target.

Furthermore, when the ball is above your feet you will naturally make a flatter backswing, and your right hand will tend to overpower your left in the hitting area. These factors combine to produce a right-to-left ball flight, and so you must aim to the right of your target to compensate for this (5:35).

5:34 If the ball is below the level of your feet at address, then the likely outcome is a shot that tends to fade away to the right of your target.

5:35 If, on the other hand, the ball lies above the level of your feet, the effect of the slope is such that the ball will tend to fly to the left of your target with hookspin.

The low, left-to-right fade
SEVE BALLESTEROS

There are two basic ways of moving the ball. On the one hand, you can develop a mechanical routine whereby you make the necessary adjustments to your set-up before you play, ie. offset the position of the clubface with the position of your body. After doing that, you swing normally. Alternatively you can learn to feel the clubhead and manufacture a shot, just as Seve illustrates here. This takes a little more time to perfect, and requires that you feel the shot in your hands, but once you learn to associate a particular shape of shot with the feeling through impact you will be able to control the flight of the ball accurately.

To play a low, left-to-right shot, Seve sets up to the ball by aiming his body to the left of his intended target, but places the clubface behind the ball square to his target line.

The swing itself is slightly more upright than normal, and his backswing position quite clearly indicates that his intention is to carve the ball low around the trees. Through impact, his overriding thought is to pull the clubface across the ball, spinning it from left to right as it is squeezed forward.

Such a cutting action necessarily forces you to make a slightly restricted follow-through, and you can see here that Seve's right arm has remained beneath his left. There has been no crossover whatsoever. When you play any left-to-right shot I would advise that you grip a little more firmly than normal with your left hand and a little easier with your right hand. This will encourage your left hand to lead the clubhead into the ball while reducing any tendency that your right hand has to roll the clubface closed at impact.

The low raking hook
SEVE BALLESTEROS

To play the low hook, the alterations that are necessary involve aiming your body to the right of your intended target line, and positioning the ball more towards the middle of your stance. In other words, you close the clubface in relation to your body alignment at address. After that, you swing normally.

The method that Seve employs in part involves making these adjustments, but instinctively he still 'feels' the shot through his hands. To hook the ball this involves encouraging the hands to be active in closing the clubface on the ball through impact. The feeling that you must have is that of your right hand being encouraged to cross over the left through impact, slinging the ball out to the right with the spin to hook it back.

In order to create that effect, Seve sets up to make a slightly flatter, more rounded swing. That enables him to really attack the ball from the inside, and in the process, helps him to roll his right hand over the left through impact. Just look at how he works his hands through impact, closing the clubface on the ball and sweeping it away with hookspin.

The follow-through position that you see here reflects the much flatter swing that he has made in order to produce such heavy hookspin. If you compare this with the corresponding position that he achieved playing the low slice, you will clearly see the difference in technique.

Putting
by Tim Barter

Just as good mechanics are vital for the sustained performance of the full swing, they are fundamental in the process of building and maintaining a sound putting stroke. The method that I teach is one that I believe will help you to develop a simple and easily repeatable putting stroke, and it is based largely upon careful observation of the world's leading professional players.

Putting is considered to be a most individual matter, and yet if we look closely at the methods that are employed by these players, we can identify a number of factors that are common to all. As we have stated before, there are certain principles that determine the way in which we all swing the golf club, and similarly, there are certain key elements that must form the foundation of any successful putting stroke.

But by its simple nature alone, the putting action is open to much personal interpretation. The huge variety of styles that we see on display is proof that putting is by far the most idiosyncratic part of the game, and by that token you must never be afraid to experiment as you fashion your own particular style. Nick Faldo and José Maria Olazabal, for example, are two of the finest putters in the world today, and yet their methods feature characteristic differences that are totally in keeping with their approach to the game in general.

Faldo, of course, is a model golfer who strikes a truly classical pose, and he wields the putter with the same ease and elegance with which he swings a driver (**6:1**). His putting stroke, like his full swing, is as orthodox as one could possibly be, and his mechanics follow the words of the textbook to the letter. Olazabal, in subtle contrast, is the more clinical of the two players, a young predator, whose sharp, aggressive style has earned him the reputation of being perhaps the deadliest putter in the world

6:1, 6:2 Nick Faldo's orthodox putting stroke follows the words of the textbook to the letter, while Olazabal, in contrast, is typically aggressive, with a much more clinical action.

6:3, 6:3a Bernhard Langer has overcome one of the cruellest afflictions in golf – the yips – with this self-styled two-handed grip, in which he clasps his left forearm against the shaft with his right hand.

from inside ten feet (**6:2**). While Faldo strokes the putts with a measured pendulum action that is controlled predominantly by the movement of his shoulders, Olazabal's style is much more hands-and-arms orientated, and he really does rap the ball into the back of the hole. Individual methods both, but each extremely effective.

Those of you who follow the professional game will no doubt be familiar with the extraordinary battle that Bernhard Langer has had with the putter. One of the game's most naturally talented players from tee to green, Langer has twice had to overcome what must surely be golf's most crippling and humbling disease – the 'yips'. That achievement has not only made him into a very fine putter, but the sheer determination with which he has fought to survive has also increased his mental toughness in every aspect of the game. With a putting action that is totally his own design (**6:3, 6:3a**), Langer has managed to maintain his position as one of the best players in the world.

But despite their obvious differences, these players – and indeed the majority of the world's leading players – do share similarities in their basic approach to putting. These similarities, or common denominators, represent what I believe to be the core fundamentals that you must learn to incorporate into your own stroke if you are serious about improving your long-term performance on the greens.

A routine approach that engenders consistency

In golf generally, but in putting particularly, the power of the mind over the body can be overwhelming. To be totally successful on the greens, it is essential that you develop the art of positive thinking and try always to be concerned with the positive aspects involved with making a putt and not worrying about all the possible ways that it could be missed. Negative thoughts, at any stage during the process of sizing up and executing a stroke, will only weaken your resolve.

Before looking more closely at the mechanics of the stroke itself, it is worth noting just how disciplined professional players are in their approach to putting, no matter what the situation. Their mental preparation involves following a set procedure, and they address each and every putt with a purpose that never varies. It is due to their ability to harness and sharply focus their concentration within such a calculated routine that they are able to withstand the enormous pressures of tournament play.

Developing a positive routine is the key to consistency. The time to begin your own mental preparation is the moment your ball arrives on the putting surface. You should then begin surveying the contours of the green, picking out the line that you intend to follow, and judging the exact pace that is required (**6:4**). Ideally, you should strive to build a mental

6:4 *First, study your putt and try to visualise the ball running towards the hole.*

6:5 *Once you are satisfied that you have chosen the right line, carefully aim the putter-face.*

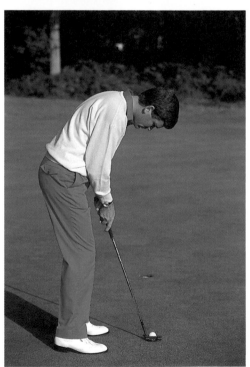

6:6 *Complete your grip, and settle down into a comfortable position over the ball.*

6:7 *Finally, make a smooth, uninhibited stroke, accelerating the putter-head towards the hole.*

picture of the ball rolling along your chosen line before disappearing into the hole.

Once you have reached a decision on the line, you must then set the face of the putter squarely to it (**6:5**). The most important fundamental of all is aim, and when the time comes to approach the ball you must carefully aim the face along the line you have chosen before completing your grip and finally settling down into a comfortable position (**6:6**).

Only when you are totally satisfied with your alignment and your posture should you attempt to make a smooth, uninhibited stroke, keeping your head still and the putter-head moving low to the ground. Accelerate through the ball and towards the hole, and hold your finish so that you can check that the face has maintained its square alignment during the stroke (**6:7**). Don't ever be defensive and try to guide the ball towards the hole, but be positive with it. Confidence is your greatest ally.

Let's now look at the fundamentals of the stroke.

The grip

The top professional players in the world putt with what I would describe as a 'palm-to-palm' grip, in which each hand assumes a neutral position on the club. If you stand with your arms hanging down by your side you should find that your hands fall into this position quite naturally, with your palms facing each other and your finger-tips pointing to the ground (**6:8, 6:8a**). Your hands should then maintain this position as they are applied to the club.

The way in which you decide to marry your hands together on the club is a matter of personal preference, and there are a number of options available. Comfort must be your prime consideration as you experiment with the possible variations before deciding on the one that best suits your particular putting style.

By far the most popular grip among professional golfers today is what's known as the 'reverse-overlap', a simple adaptation of the Vardon grip, in which the left forefinger rides outside the fingers of the right hand (**6:9, 6:9a**). While some players hook this finger underneath and around the grip, others prefer to point it straight down the shaft, so that it rests along the back of the first three fingers of the right hand. Again, it's purely a matter of comfort. To promote a good, square alignment, the pads of each thumb should lie on top of the grip, while simply crooking the right forefinger under the shaft will serve to heighten your sense of feel and control.

The reverse-overlap grip is favoured by better players because it provides essential support in the back of the left wrist, and that suits their putting philosophy. It helps to promote a positive, firm-wristed action through impact. As the left wrist is denied the opportunity to

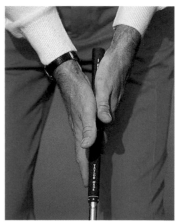

6:8, 6:8a *With a palm-to-palm grip, each hand assumes a neutral position on the club.*

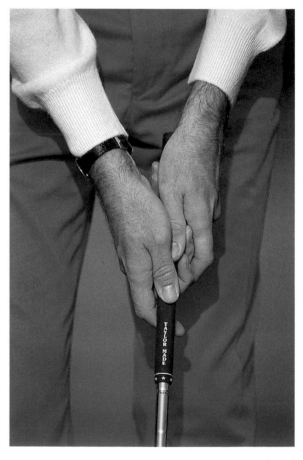

6:9, 6:9a *Comfort must be your prime consideration as you marry your hands together on the grip. The majority of professional players favour the reverse-overlap grip, in which the left forefinger rides outside the fingers of the right hand.*

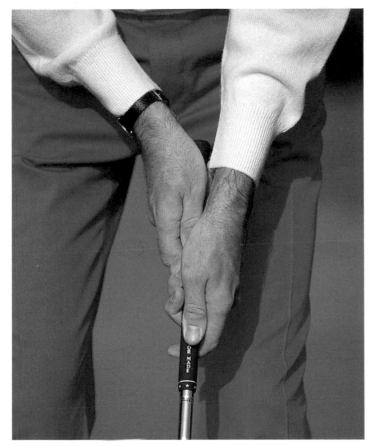

6:10 The cross-handed grip, in which the left hand is placed below the right, is a popular alternative for those players wanting to guard against excessive wrist action.

collapse, the reverse-overlap grip encourages a stroke that keeps the putter-head moving low to the ground, and makes a consistent contact with the ball.

But while it's true that the hands work very much as a unit, they do also have individual responsibilities. I believe that the left hand is largely responsible for the directional elements of the stroke, while the right assumes a greater degree of responsibility for feel.

I would advise everyone to at least experiment with the reverse-overlap grip, and develop a stroke that features as little wrist action as possible. But if it proves to be uncomfortable, then switch to either

the more conventional Vardon hold, the interlocking grip, or even a ten-finger 'baseball' grip if that feels more comfortable. Another alternative is the cross-handed grip, in which the left hand is placed below the right (**6:10**). This has proved to be very popular among players who feel that they need a little extra insurance against unwanted wrist action through impact, and it leads to a solid pendulum stroke that is controlled predominantly by the left hand.

Whatever your decision, make sure that your grip feels comfortable, and that it affords you a good sense of feel. Think about your grip pressure. Don't grip the

6:11, 6:11a, 6:12 For the desired upward brushing stroke through impact, the ball should be played somewhere between the middle of your stance and the inside of your left heel.

putter so tightly that you lose all sense of the head on the end of the shaft, but don't hold it so loosely that you sacrifice control. A light, sensitive grip, with even pressure in both hands, will probably serve you best.

Ball position

One of the few rules that you must follow when preparing to putt is that which concerns your ball position. The ball should be placed somewhere between the centre of your stance and the inside of your left heel (**6:11, 6:11a**). Not only will this allow you to view the line of your putt to the hole with the greatest ease, but a forward position will encourage the desired upward brushing stroke through impact (**6:12**). If the ball is played too far back in your stance, it is quite likely that your backswing will be steep and the downswing path into the ball too sharp

*:13 A ball played too far back in the
tance will create a stroke that is much
oo steep, with inconsistent results.*

*6:14 Check your ball position in relation to
your eye-line by simply dropping a ball from
the bridge of your nose.*

(6:13). This will often cause the ball to 'hop' as it leaves the putter, creating an inconsistent roll on the green.

It is also important that you set your sights correctly at address, and consider the position of the ball in relation to your eye-line. Ideally, your eyes should be set directly over the ball-target line; indeed many of the world's best players stand with their eyes directly above the ball. You must certainly never stand so that your eye-line falls outside the ball-target line. That would greatly distort your view to the hole, and can lead to you not only misreading the line of your putts, but often mis-hitting the ball.

Check your ball position on a regular basis. You can do this quite simply by setting up to a putt normally, and then dropping a ball from the bridge of your nose to indicate its exact position on the ground in relation to your eye-line

6:15 Try to assemble a fairly tall position at address, and let your arms hang comfortably in front of you. Your shoulders exert the greatest influence on the path of your stroke, and so it's imperative that they run parallel with the ball-target line.

(**6:14**). Alternatively, use a mirror on the ground and determine the position of your eyes in relation to the ball in the reflection.

Body alignment and posture

Tournament players tend to favour a firm-wristed putting action within a fairly mechanical framework, in which movement is restricted to the hands, arms and shoulders. The uncertainty that too much wrist and hand action can bring to a putting stroke is thus eliminated, as the movement is controlled predominantly by the shoulders. For this pendulum-like stroke to work effectively it is vital that the body is first positioned correctly.

You should work around a square address position, because it is much easier to develop a consistent putting stroke from this base. Ideally you should stand with your feet, knees, hips and shoulders all square to the line of your putt. Try to assume a fairly tall position, and let your arms hang freely and comfortably in front of you. But if you do find that a slightly open stance is more comfortable, then by all means work around that, but a word of caution. Your shoulders exert the greatest influence on the path of your putting stroke, and so it's imperative that they run parallel with the ball-target line (**6:15**).

For the pendulum action to work consistently, your posture must allow your arms complete freedom of movement. A crouched position only serves to restrict the ease with which the arms and shoulders can control the stroke, and generally leads to a more wristy action.

As long as you stand correctly, it should be possible to view your line by simply swivelling your head to the left. Don't fall into the habit of lifting your head to study the line of your putt to the hole. If you do that you will pull your whole body out of position, and make it very difficult to re-establish the correct set-up.

Building pendulum motion from the shoulders

Once you have a good grip and set-up, the putting stroke can be regarded as a simple shoulder movement. There should be nothing complicated about it at all. From a mechanical point of view, the key elements of alignment and positioning have already been satisfied, and now it is simply a case of setting your pendulum stroke in motion.

One of the best ways in which you can build a pendulum stroke is to trap an old shaft across your chest, making sure that it is parallel with the ball-target line, and then keep it there as you make a stroke (**6:16, 6:17, 6:18**). Feel the connection between your arms and shoulders. The triangle that is formed by the arms and shoulders at address is perfectly maintained as the stroke is controlled with a gentle rocking motion from the shoulders, and the putter-head is kept low to the ground as it follows a consistent path towards the hole. Your stroke should be smooth, and slightly accelerating through impact. Feel the strike as being slightly upwards, and aim

inside the target-line in the backswing (**6:19**), and then returning to a square position at impact before moving inside once more in the follow-through (**6:20**). The overall length of your backswing

to make contact at, or just slightly below, the middle of the ball.

As long as the shoulders work up and down in plane, the putter-head will trace a natural path, running slightly

should be governed strictly by the length of your putt.

On the subject of path, it is important that you understand that the putter-head does not follow a straight line back-and-through to the hole. That's a common misconception that must be dismissed. While it might be possible to follow a relatively straight line back-and-through towards the target on the shorter putts, let's say putts of up to six or seven feet, simple geometry dictates that as the length of the stroke increases the putter-head must move progressively further inside the ball-target line. The putter-face should remain square to the path along which it is swinging, despite the fact that the putter-head moves inside the ball-target line (**6:21**).

The pendulum stroke is one that is essentially designed to eliminate wrist action, although on the longer putts you will find that you do need to introduce a certain amount of wrist action in order to create the clubhead speed necessary to get

6:16, 6:17, 6:18
The connection between your arms and shoulders that characterizes the pendulum stroke can be felt immediately if you trap an old shaft across your chest, and keep it there as you move the putter to and fro.

6:19 As long as the shoulders work up and down in plane, the putter-head will trace a natural path, running slightly inside the target-line in the backswing, and then returning to a square position at impact.

6:20, 6:21 For a consistent strike, try to keep the putter moving low to the ground through the ball, and hold your finish so that you can check to make sure that the putter-face has remained on line.

the ball to the hole. Accuracy from a short range is dependent upon a mechanically sound, clinical action, but consistently successful long putting is much more dependent upon feel, and adding just a suspicion of wrist action will heighten your sense of feel for distance, and help you to develop a fluent, free-flowing stroke towards the hole. Although it may be possible to generate sufficient clubhead speed with a much shorter stroke, there is always the danger of that stroke becoming jerky, with the obvious consequence of inconsistent striking.

Your putting strategy

The better the mechanics of your stroke, the better putter you are likely to be. That's why in the long term, practice is so vital. But as I mentioned earlier, putting is a game that is played very much in the mind, and so your strategy is just as important as the physical elements within your stroke in determining your success.

To be a consistently good putter you must learn to gather information. As you approach a green look for clues that will help you to determine both the pace and the line of your putt. Look out for areas of high ground and try to build up an overall picture of the green's make-up. The experience of playing on many different types of course will teach you the subtle differences you will face.

Use all the time that you have between shots efficiently. Study your own putt while your partners play, and wherever possible 'go to school' on their efforts, and learn from the behaviour of their ball as it approaches the hole. Greens will often vary in pace from one hole to the next, and simply watching your opponent or partner putt first could save you from making an unnecessary error in judgement. Always be alert.

There should be a difference in your approach to long and short putts. Whenever you are a long way from the hole, you should think in terms of taking no more than two putts to get down. Imagine the ball dying next to the hole, so that you leave yourself a simple tap-in. Most three-putts are the result of poor distance judgement rather than careless direction. So think hard about pace. Make a couple of long, smooth practice swings, and keep the putter-head swinging freely towards the hole. Then stroke the ball smoothly across the green. Whenever you face a putt with a considerable break, make sure that you err on the high side of the hole when determining your line. If the slope is left-to-right, then keep the ball running towards the hole from the high side to the left. Then the ball has a chance of falling in as it slows. But if you miss on the low side, the ball isn't going to swerve and run uphill. Always give the ball a chance to go in.

Short putting is all about accuracy, and developing a clinical and precise method. Pace is obviously still important, but you can hit a putt of four feet too hard and the ball will still go in if it is dead on line. A good short putter is usually very positive with his stroke from within four or five feet of the hole, because he is not worried about having to face the putt coming back should he miss.

The pace at which you strike your putts from close range will depend to a certain extent upon the situation that you are in. If you are playing a match, and face a tricky short putt for a half, then you might as well be positive and strike the ball firmly into the back of the cup. But in a stroke-play situation, when every single stroke counts, you must think very carefully before being overly bold.

The few minutes that you spend on the putting green before a round are very important. The worst thing you can do before a game is drop a few balls just a few feet away from the hole and then miss each and every one. Following a succession of misses your confidence hits rock bottom and you immediately put yourself under pressure. Try not to become too 'hole conscious'. Practise without a hole for a while. Pick out some other target and just try to get a feel for the putter, a feel for your stroke and some idea of the pace of the greens that day. Then move on to a few short ones, just a foot or so from the hole, and get used to the sound of the ball falling in. Holing a number of short putts in succession before you go out gives you a positive mental attitude, and confidence is everything.

Putting drills for accuracy and feel

Throughout this chapter, I've made a number of references to the world's leading players, to the key elements that characterize their putting strokes and to their positive routine which helps them sustain such a high level of performance. The final reference that I would like to make is one that is perhaps the most pertinent of all. It is simply that they practise relentlessly. Professional golfers spend more time on the putting green than they do anywhere else, and that's why they are so good.

To practise is your very best strategy. Here are some drills to help make the most of your practice sessions.

1. Board drill

One of the best ways to condition a repeating stroke for short putts is the parallel board drill (**6:22, 6:22a**). This exercise requires you to find a dead-straight putt of three or four feet on your practice green and then, as I have done here, place two boards on the ground running parallel to the target-line with the ball positioned between them.

The boards should be just far enough apart so that your putter-head fits between them with, say, half an inch

6:22, 6:22a The board drill will help you to develop an accurate, repeating stroke from close range.

clearance on either side. Each board will then act as a guide, and train you to produce a relatively straight-back and straight-through stroke. If your stroke is true, you should be able to glide your putter back and through to the hole without touching either board.

A word of warning. This drill is only designed to match your putting stroke from close range. It builds a straight-back and straight-through action that is ideal from three or four feet and under. As you move further away from the hole, you stroke will obviously get longer, and move progressively further inside the ball-target line.

2. Ladder drill

From short range the emphasis is on accuracy. You can test the reliability of your short-putting stroke by placing five or six balls in a straight line, the first about eighteen inches from the hole, the second at two feet, then three feet and so on, and then holing them one by one (**6:23**). Begin with the ball closest to the hole, and gradually work back. As each putt gets longer your stroke will need to be slightly longer, still making sure that it remains accurate. You could even introduce an element of pressure, and set yourself a target. Challenge your stroke and find out just how many putts you can

6:24 Test your versatility with the star drill, this time placing the balls around a hole and approaching each putt afresh.

6:23 Test the reliability of your stroke with the ladder drill, gradually increasing the length of each putt as you move away from the hole.

hole in succession. Eventually it becomes a test of nerve.

3. Star drill

The star drill is similar to the ladder drill, in that it tests the reliability of your stroke from close range, but it also tests your versatility, as each putt will be from a different angle (**6:24**). Moving around the hole in this way forces you to approach each putt afresh, and so helps to establish a routine for alignment and posture. If you should miss before completing the circle, then go back to the first ball and start all over again.

Place the balls around a hole that is cut on fairly level ground, but as you become more ambitious, move to a hole that lies on an obvious slope. Then you

will be tested to the full, faced with a downhill putt, an uphill putt, a left-to-right breaking putt and a right-to-left putt. Gradually increase the distance you place the balls from the hole, and again, test your nerve by setting a target and then trying to beat it.

4. Random targets for feel

Good short putting is very much about making a reliable stroke and popping the ball firmly into the back of the hole. Long putting is far more a question of having a good sense of feel, being able to judge the distance that is required and then stroking the ball a dead-weight to the hole.

Although your stroke will essentially remain the same, varying the distance to each target as you practise will

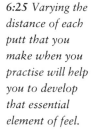

6:25 Varying the distance of each putt that you make when you practise will help you to develop that essential element of feel.

6:26 *Another way to test your feel is to putt a number of balls with your eyes closed. Roll your first putt to the distance of fifteen feet or so, and then try to roll each subsequent ball as close to the first as possible.*

gradually teach you the relationship between the length of swing and pace. In other words it's a great way to develop feel (**6:25**).

5. Close your eyes for greater awareness

When you lose one of your senses, the others automatically sharpen up to compensate, and this provides us with another useful exercise with which to develop feel.

    With four or five balls, simply putt the first to a distance of fifteen feet or so, and then with each subsequent ball, but with your eyes closed, try to cluster them all together as tightly as possible (**6:26**). Closing your eyes before you putt should immediately heighten your feel for the putter-head in your fingertips, hands and arms, and with a clear picture of the putt in your mind, you will be surprised at just how closely you are able to group the balls together.

6. Gate Drill

This exercise will not only help you to appreciate the importance of reading the line of a putt which features a significant borrow, but it will teach you the importance of judging pace. The line and pace of any putt are inversely related, and it is important that you learn the effect that pace has on the behaviour of a ball across a slope. Find a putt that features a significant borrow, and place two tees in the ground so that they form a gate along the ideal line of the putt (**6:27**). This is now your target. If you hit the ball too hard it will fail to break sufficiently and miss the gate, and the hole, on the high

6:27 *The line and the pace of any putt are, of course, related, and this gate exercise can help you to gauge the behaviour of the ball as it runs across a slope.*

6:28, 6:28a *Another way in which you can learn the relationship between the line and the pace of a putt is to set out a number of balls from a hole following the line of break for about twenty yards. Start with the ball closest to the hole and move back, learning all the time from the previous putt.*

side; hit the putt too softly and the ball will take too much borrow and trickle away from the hole on the low side.

7. Visualize the line

Another way in which you can learn the relationship between the line and the pace of a putt is to set out a number of balls from a hole following the line of break for about twenty yards. The balls will form a curve, and illustrate for you the line to the hole (**6:28, 6:28a**).

Begin with the ball closest to the hole, and tap it in. Then, move back to the second, then the third, fourth and so on. As you move away from the hole the break of the putt will become gradually more significant and you will need to think about the pace at which you strike the ball as well as the line itself. Don't expect to hole all of these putts, but practise to develop your awareness of the relationship between line and pace.

The pendulum putting stroke
NICK FALDO

Over the last few years, so much attention has been given to Nick Faldo's swing changes under the watchful eye of David Leadbetter that it is at times easy to lose sight of the fact that as well as being one of the game's most accurate ball strikers, Faldo is also one of the finest putters in the world.

His style on the greens illustrates perfectly the simplicity of the basic pendulum stroke. With a putter that is three-quarters of an inch shorter than standard, Faldo, who is 6'3" tall, stands to the ball with his arms hanging comfortably down, and the putter immediately becomes an extension of his body. He looks to be at ease and in total command at address, and his stroke is all the more effective as a result.

Faldo putts with a stance that is approximately the width of his shoulders, and to create the desired upward brushing stroke through impact, he positions the ball approximately two inches inside his left heel. Like so many professionals today, Faldo prefers to use the reverse-overlap grip when putting, and his hands fall comfortably into position above the ball.

For the pendulum stroke to be effective, the shoulders must be aligned parallel with the ball-to-target line, and while Faldo often experiments with a slightly open stance, his shoulders (and indeed his hips) are perfectly positioned. Once he is totally satisfied that the putter-face is square to his target-line, and that his body is accordingly aligned, the stroke is made with a simple rocking motion that is controlled by the shoulders. The putter head traces a path that moves progressively to the inside of the ball-to-target line as the length of the stroke increases, and through the ball Faldo keeps the blade on line, and his head still until the ball is on its way towards the hole.

A most noticeable feature of Faldo's style is that his hands remain passive throughout. Only on a long putt do you detect a slight break in the wrists, and it is because he is able to control the angle that he creates at the back of his wrists at address during the stroke that he is so accurate. Excessive wrist action is often the killer of a sound putting stroke, but as Faldo illustrates, the pendulum stroke eliminates it totally.

Strategy
by Tommy Horton

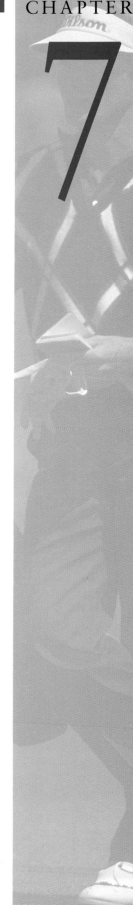

In chapter two I made the observation that every golf swing is different. So it follows that how those swings are used will differ from golfer to golfer. Every one has different strengths, weaknesses and tendencies. And nowhere is that more important than when it comes to strategy, or course management as the professionals like to call it.

Knowing how to manage your swing and your emotions on the course is a big part of golf. Someone who has a good swing and can hit the ball well is not necessarily a golfer in the fullest sense of the word. There is more to it than that. Most of it lies inside your head. Knowing what you are and are not capable of at any given moment can make or save your score. In short, never let your expectations exceed your capabilities.

To find out which strategy is best for you, you have to ask yourself a basic question. Why do you play golf? Is it to know the thrill of hitting three tee shots

miles down the middle, or do you actually want to complete the round in as few strokes as possible? If you fall into the former category, this chapter is probably not going to be of much help to you. If the ability to hit three great shots a round outweighs the frustration of thirty poor shots, keep playing the way you've always played. Just don't bet too much money.

If you are genuinely interested in getting around the course in as efficient a manner as possible, read on. This chapter is for you.

Mental mistakes can be just as costly as a bad swing at the wrong time. For example, how many times have you seen a good score ruined by someone attempting a shot which offers maybe a one-in-a-thousand chance of success? Attacking golf is all very well, I'm all for it in the right circumstances, but make realism the fifteenth club in your bag. Golf is a lot easier played from the fairway.

7:1 The cavaliering go-for-broke philosophy of Arnold Palmer is thrilling for his army of fans, but it is rarely the strategy that you should pursue out on the course.

Not everyone is an Arnold Palmer any more than they are a Nick Faldo. They've both done pretty well with fundamentally different philosophies on how the game should be played. Palmer is a man who will go for the flag in almost any situation. He knows only one way to play: at full-throttle (**7:1**).

For that reason he has had both spectacular victories and stunning defeats. Look at his record in the US Masters. Arnold won at Augusta in 1960 by scoring birdies at the final two holes to beat Ken Venturi by a shot. Then the very next year he came up the 18th fairway needing a par to win and took six to lose by one. He lived and died by his ability to bring off difficult shots under the severest pressure.

The approach of a Nick Faldo, on the other hand, is much closer to the one I would recommend for you (**7:2**). He changes gears to suit the occasion a little more than Arnold ever did. His play over the last few holes of the British Open at St Andrews in 1990 illustrates my point perfectly. Four or five shots ahead, there was no need for Nick to try anything too fancy. So he didn't. He played sensible, conservative golf, particularly at the very dangerous Road Hole. Nick did not flirt at all with the Road Bunker. He knew he could run up a seven or eight from in there. So he played safely short, and right of the green. That made anything more than a five unlikely. He could pitch safely up the length of the green and maybe hole

7:2 The cool, calculated approach of Nick Faldo is, by comparison to a player of Palmer's style, perhaps not that exciting, but his record more than makes up for that.

7:3 Sacrificing a few extra yards for greater accuracy will always pay dividends, as this ten yard drill will teach you. The next time that you play, whenever you hit your tee shot into the rough, pick the ball up and replace it ten yards further back but in the middle of the fairway. As I'm sure that your scorecard will reveal, position beats distance in the long run.

the putt for par. But even if he didn't a five was all right.

Make that your approach. Follow the old maxim. 'If you have two shots in hand, use them'. Look at it this way. The average player's handicap is around 19. That tells me that the average player is not competent enough to hit the fairway with a driver 80 per cent of the time. He would be much better off hitting a 3- or even a 5-wood from the tee. His ball will go almost as far and finish in play a lot more often. And, more importantly, his score at the end of the round will be lower.

Try this 'ten yard' drill if you are in any doubt (7:3). Whenever you hit your tee shot into the rough or into a hazard,

pick the ball up and place it ten yards further back but in the middle of the fairway. It's my bet that your score will be at least six strokes below your handicap. Proof indeed that position beats distance in the long run.

Position beats distance is never more applicable than on holes where you cannot reach the green in two shots. Take a long par-5 for example, a hole that measures well over 500 yards that is out of range in two shots to all but the longest hitters (7:4). With that in mind, why would you ever hit a driver from the tee? You know you cannot reach the green in two, so why make things more difficult than they already are? I'd rather hit two easy shots than two difficult ones if all

7:4 The first rule of good course management is to always err on the conservative side. If, for example, you face a long par-5 that is out of range in two shots, but comfortably reached in three, then why make the hole more difficult than it need be by taking a driver from the tee. Your objective should be to put yourself in the ideal position in two shots to attack the pin with your third, and invariably a 3-wood or even a 5-wood from the tee will make your task much easier.

I'm going to get at the end is a slightly longer third shot. That is the first rule of good course management: if in doubt, err on the conservative side.

There is little point in attacking this hole from the tee. A bad drive can lead to a lost ball either right or left in the sandhills. There is no recovering from that; back to the tee you go. I liken the player who thoughtlessly blasts away with his driver to the long jumper who expects a personal best every time. It cannot be done, so don't try it.

Tee off with the club you know is likely to put you in play. That can be your 3-wood, 5-wood or 1-iron. Knowing before you start that your prospects are good increases the likelihood of you hitting a good shot. You gain confidence from the knowledge that you are doing something well within your capabilities. Panic only sets in when you are not sure what lies ahead.

Having found the fairway, your next step is to avoid trouble. Know how far it is to that bunker or the trees or the water short of the green and play a club you *know* will see you safely short. Then you can use the hazard as a target. When you decide to play short, make sure you do.

If you do get into tree trouble, don't make the mistake I see so many amateurs make. They decide to play safely back into the fairway without trying anything too outrageous. That's good but then they reach automatically for the wedge. That means trouble because a wedge is a lofted club designed to get the ball up in the air quickly. If you are in a clump of trees surrounded by overhanging branches, the last thing you want is a high-flying shot. So take a straight-faced club and punch the ball out *under* the branches. A simple point, but one much abused (**7:5, 7:5a**).

Use your approach shot as a way of bringing the strength of your game into play. Say you're a terrific wedge player. Try to hit the ball a wedge distance from the hole. If you are less than confident with the wedge, play less club on your second shot so that you can hit a longer approach.

Either way, avoid your weaknesses by playing to your strengths.

You may think that this is a very conservative style of play. I beg to differ. This is aggressive golf. The best golfers find ways to hit the shots they hit best. They greatly increase their chances of a short birdie putt by playing their approach shots with a club in which they have confidence. Top American money winner Tom Kite is the master of this. Tom is not a long hitter, but he scores a lot of birdies on par five holes despite sacrificing yardage. He knows that he can hit his sand wedge 70 yards time after time, so he tries to be 70 yards from the hole after two shots (**7:6**). Not 60 or 80 yards but 70 yards. He treats golf like a game of chess and so should you. Plot your way round the course. Have a game

7:5, 7:5a If you do find yourself with tree-trouble, then bear in mind that reaching for the wedge to play out to safety is not always the wise thing to do. Designed to get the ball up into the air quickly, your wedge could put you in even more trouble if the ball strikes one of the over-hanging branches. So remember to take a straight-faced club, and punch the ball out under the branches to safety.

7:6 Tom Kite is an example of a player who plays specifically to his stengths. Tom is not a long hitter, but he makes a lot of birdies on par-5 holes simply because he is a great wedge player from 70 yards, and so tries to leave himself that distance from the green whenever possible with his approach shot.

plan and stick to it as far as possible. Constantly ask yourself: 'Where do I want to be when I come to play my next shot?'

Talk of yardage brings us to the next step in course management. Know the distance you commonly hit each club. That can only help you plot your strategy for each hole or each round. If you don't know how far you are likely to hit a certain club, then even some of your good shots are going to get you into trouble.

Go to the practice ground with twenty balls. Take your 7-iron. Hit twenty shots but disregard the longest five and the shortest five. The middle ten balls represent your average shot length (7:7). Measure to the centre of the group and that gives you a good idea as to how far you can expect to hit your 7-iron. Do the same exercise for each club.

A word of caution about yardages. Don't overestimate their importance. Don't be a slave to your notebook. Yardages are useful, but they are merely a starting point. Rarely will you be able to base your club selection purely on the yardage involved. Why do you think most club golfers come up short of the hole on the vast majority of their approach shots? They don't take enough account of the other variables involved. Wind, the terrain and the lie of the ball all play a part in your final decision. Yardages are useful but not the decisive factor.

If you feel that you may be guilty of consistent under-clubbing, test yourself. Record where your shots to the green finish over an extended period, say five rounds. Don't be surprised if you are short seven times out of ten. That's normal but remember your tendency next time you are standing over an approach shot. Take one club more and aim for the back of the green. It can be surprisingly difficult to hit your ball too far. Most bunkers and water hazards are placed in front of the green so being too long is not a bad option.

Practise your course management away from the course. That may sound peculiar, but thinking clearly about your game is easier away from the tensions and stresses of competition. As much as the driving range or practice ground is the place to hone your swing, your lounge at home is the place to put your mind in order.

Let me caddie for you

A good caddie can be worth a couple of shots a round to a top professional. Nick Faldo went as far as replacing Andy Prodger with Fanny Sunesson at the beginning of 1990 because he felt their relationship was not quite right, and look how well he has done since (7:8).

Obviously you are not going to rush out and get yourself a caddie, but the sooner you start thinking like one, the sooner you can eliminate some of your more careless shots. I have long felt that I could turn an average 19 handicap player into a 14 handicap player without touching his golf swing. Simply by telling

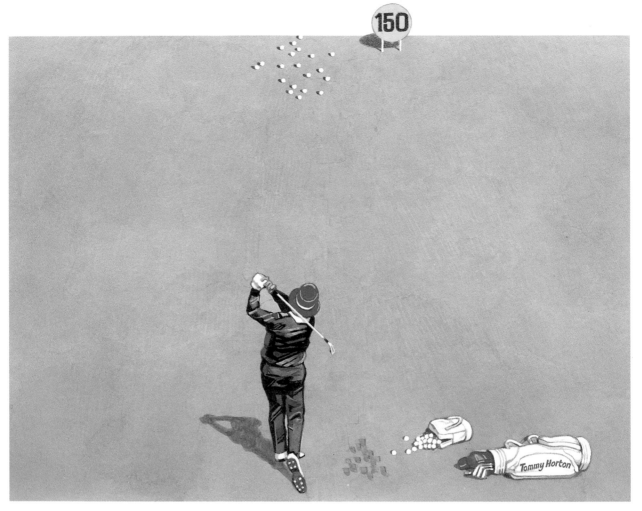

150

7:7 Knowing the distance that you hit each club in your bag is essential if you are going to reap the full benefits of course management.

him what club to play and when to play it, I could save at least five shots per round.

Rarely would I allow my player to take a driver from the tee. That club would put him in trouble more often than not. So it's a 3- or 5-wood from the tee. His long irons would gather dust in the bag along with the driver. Handicap golfers think only in terms of distance when what they really should be paying attention to is trajectory. Long irons are tough to hit up in the air. Shots hit with them tend to fly in low and run a long way on landing. That is all right some of the time, but has limited usefulness if

there is any trouble ahead. For that reason, a 5-wood is much better than a 3-iron. It is a more forgiving club. Even a slight mis-hit will get the ball airborne.

Around the greens is where I could save the most shots. Too many players I see in pro-ams are obsessed with height when chipping and pitching. They use their sand wedges or wedges from everywhere, even just off the green with nothing between them and the hole. The only time you want to put the ball in the air when chipping or pitching is when you have to. Far better to take a 7- or 8-iron and knock the ball along the ground if you can. That type of shot gives you more margin for error and is really only an extension of a long putt.

A good caddie can be a godsend in other areas too. Knowing when to speak, when not to speak and how fast or slow to walk can make the difference between winning and losing. Maybe Greg Norman wouldn't have won the 1986 British Open if his caddie hadn't told him to slow down as he charged up the seventh hole on the last day after a badly hooked drive. Maybe Tony Lema wouldn't have won the Open at St Andrews in 1964 if he hadn't had Arnold Palmer's regular caddie, Tip Anderson, carrying his bag.

Maybe Sandy Lyle wouldn't have won in 1985 at Sandwich without the calming influence of his caddie, Dave Musgrove.

That's speculation, but the point is the same. Whenever you find yourself under pressure, or feel that your swing is getting away from you, make yourself your caddie. Try to distance yourself from the shot. Imagine what you would say to your best friend if he found himself in the position you are in at that moment. Then take your own advice. It's invariably the best.

Within your own capabilities, challenge yourself whenever you get the

7:8 The support and encouragement that a good caddy provides can be an invaluable source of inspiration for the player, as Nick Faldo has found since he was joined by Fanny Sunesson.

chance. See how good you can be. Try different shots, so that you have a better idea of just what you can do in any given situation. For example, be more specific. Don't settle for 'pretty good'. Try to hole chip shots rather than just getting them close. That philosophy works more often than you think. At the 71st hole of the 1982 US Open Tom Watson chipped in from behind the green after his caddie had told him. 'Just get this close'. Watson's reaction was, 'Close? I'm going to hole it'. And, of course, he did (**7:9**).

How to practise

I know you've heard this before: constructive practice is your quickest route to better golf. You can sit and read this book all you want, but you still have to put in some work if you want to improve appreciably.

There are two types of practice.

You can either be organised or aimless. Aimless practice is just exercise. It is not intelligent at all. So you need a programme, a plan of attack, before you begin.

Start with a few practice swings, just to loosen up your golf muscles. You don't see athletes starting to run or jump without warming up and stretching first, so neither should you. And don't just make any old swing. Pick out a spot on the ground at which you can aim. A weed, a divot, anything. Just be sure that you are trying to *hit* something. That's what you'll be doing later, after all.

Once you're ready to hit some shots, aim at a target about fifty yards away. Begin with some easy, half-wedge shots (**7:10**). Feel your swing without worrying too much where the ball is finishing. Try to picture a shot on a particular hole while you hit each ball. This will focus your attention on the job at hand.

Move steadily through the bag, hitting a few shots with each club (**7:11**, **7:12**). This achieves two things; you will establish a feel with each club and a shot pattern will emerge. If you are warming up before teeing off, play with that shot pattern. If your shots are straying a little left, allow for that out on the course. In other words, play with what you've got and don't fight it.

A genuine practice session is different. Then you can work on your mechanics more. Without the pressure of putting numbers on cards, you can experiment. That doesn't mean you react to every shot by fiddling with your swing. Don't think, 'That one went left I'll fix that'. Inevitably the next one goes right, then the one after goes left again and so on. The result is usually confusion. So wait until a trend emerges before making a change.

You can practise on the course, too. If there aren't many people about, play games against yourself. Play one ball against another. Nick Faldo, I know, does this in some of his practice rounds. He is a little more sophisticated in that he plays

7:10 It is important that you try to begin your practice session with a few short pitch shots. Pick out a target at a distance of about fifty yards and start with half-a-dozen easy wedge shots.

7:11, 7:12 As you warm up, move steadily through the bag, hitting a few shots with each club. If you are getting ready to play a round, then work specifically on your rhythm and tempo. Once you get a good feel for the clubhead with the mid-irons you can move on to the long irons and finally the woods.

fade against draw, but the principle is the same. He is attempting to recreate the feeling he has in competition. And so should you.

Get as far from your practice ground mentality as possible. Don't give yourself a second chance. On the range there is always another ball you can hit. On the course, you have to generate success in increments of one. There are no prizes for hitting five great shots then one out-of-bounds. Try to get to the stage where your bad shot finishes just off the fairway or on the edge of the green. Remember the old adage: 'Your score is determined not by the quality of your good shots, but by the quality of your bad ones'.

Don't neglect your short game either. The majority of your shots are played from less than 100 yards from the flag, so spend at least half of your practice time on and around the green. It's not as glamorous, but it's the fastest way I know to real improvement.